THEY
DON'T
TEACH
THIS AT
SCHOOL

For my children,
so you'll always be okay.

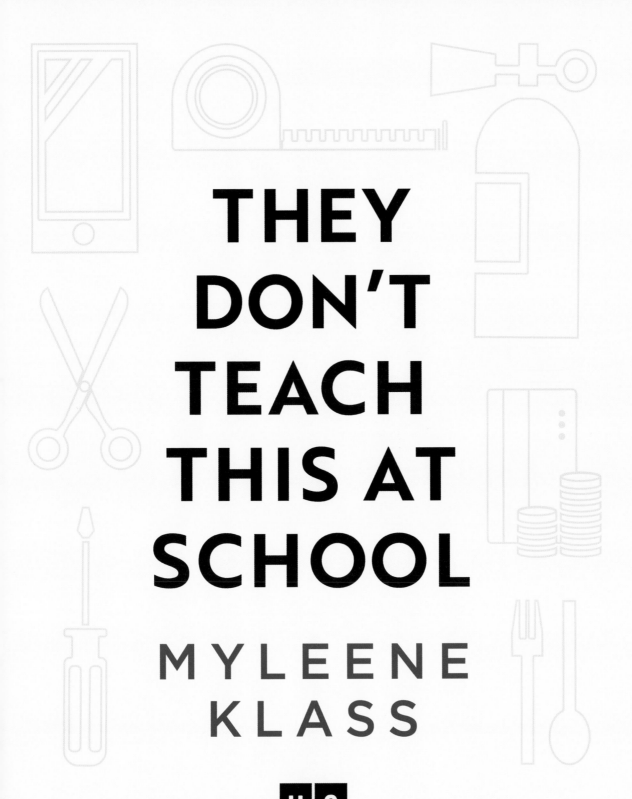

THEY DON'T TEACH THIS AT SCHOOL

MYLEENE KLASS

HQ

Introduction

'They didn't teach this at school.'

How many times have you said that? More importantly, how many times have you wished that they had?

We learned about Pythagoras, the cells of a plant, how to analyse prose, but there were huge gaps. If it wasn't in the curriculum, we missed it out. Then we went out into the world and were expected to know how to budget for a household, set up a bank account, send an invoice, call someone when the boiler broke or the taps leaked, understand when people became toxic, or our kids needed help online. We were just expected to know everything.

I was raised by a Navy dad and a mum who worked as an NHS nurse. Due to the nature of my dad's job, he was away for long periods of time, so from an early age he taught me how to help around the house when he was absent. I don't mean clearing the plates away after dinner. I mean relighting the pilot light when the boiler was down, putting oil in the car, wallpapering and decorating the house, bleeding radiators, carving chicken.

I didn't think anything of it at the time but now, living the life
I do, having raised my children as a single mum for many years
and now heading up a blended family of seven while also holding
down a career, I am so grateful for my practical, if unconventional,
upbringing - reliant on it in fact.

The worst thing anyone can ever feel is helpless. It's frustrating when
you don't know what to do or don't have the power to do something.

I wanted to write this book and share how we get through it all
in my household.

My girls don't bat an eyelid when they have to find the fuse box
when the power trips. Both have had ledgers since they were
5 years old, so they can write down their earnings and formulate
an invoice. I did this because, as a woman in the workplace,
I know just how hard it can be to ask for what is owed and then
get it. I want my children to feel empowered every step of the
way and know their worth. I have raised them to be strong in their
bodies and minds, and capable. For example, Ava has seven piano
students. I have never given her pocket money. Her money is
all hers.

I also wanted to raise my girls to be enabled, independent
(especially financially) and, ultimately, confident.

When you have information,
you have the tools you need.
This is what this book is – a toolkit
for life, full of the skills they didn't
teach you in the classroom.

We do 'fire musters' in my house, just like my dad used to do when away at sea … and then at home. I used to hate doing them as a kid as they would happen at 4 a.m. for the shock factor and general discombobulation. Now here I am doing them in my own house (not at 4 a.m.!), because although the thought of fire is scary, the actuality of it would be worse. Whenever we go to a concert or hotel, we identify all the exits and meeting points.

The girls change light bulbs, batteries, even door handles for me. They know their way around a car, how to check the oil, the tyre pressures and how to manage a household budget – something that some of my adult friends still struggle with.

Life throws so much at us. Having the basic skillset at your fingertips to survive these challenges can make all the difference. It feels positive to be arming the next generation, helping them stand on their own two feet, providing them with not what to think but how to think for themselves and so, be able to adapt and get out of tricky situations.

I've travelled the world and been in all kinds of situations myself on NGO trips and through my work as a broadcaster, and have used many of these skills and not felt vulnerable. Indeed, I have felt decidedly capable. And, as a result of these skills, I have saved not one life, but two – both of whom just happened to be my own daughters.

I hope this book – your toolkit for life – informs and empowers both you and your tribe.

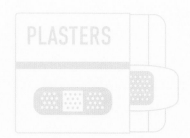

PLASTERS

Body
& soul

Family time: good for the soul

Get outside. Ava and Hero, aged 9 and 6

I taught my partner, Sim, how to plait hair. Here's his first attempt on me

Get outside and exercise whenever you can

My first job out of college as a chorus girl in *Miss Saigon* – the start of my financial independence

Never cut your own fringe

Stop blonde hair from turning green in the pool

Get a good night's sleep. I often fall asleep in the make-up chair on shoots

Always take your make-up off before bed. Hero, aged 4

Respect boundaries. Notice written by Ava, aged 6

Keep your body strong and healthy. Hero, aged 7

Get a good night's sleep

This is a subject very close to my heart. In the past I've slept through an earthquake and a fire alarm in a hotel – to the point where the fire brigade hammered on my door to wake me up! But since having children I always find myself sleeping with one ear open and I have no idea what that total oblivion, the way I see my teenage daughter sleep, feels like any more.

All those things my parents used to say about getting enough sleep are true! It's only now I have kids of my own that I realize that going to bed early is actually a pleasure not a punishment. One of my kids is a great sleeper, while one is shocking: she wanders the house like a spectre, is super-charged all the time, and sees sleep as punishment. No matter what time she goes to bed, she's always wide awake by 6.30a.m. But she needs sleep, just as we all need sleep. I know that if I've had a decent night the next day will be so much better, and it's the same for them. They might not thank me for it, but then nobody's going to thank me if they are tired and grumpy.

If you don't sleep the knock-on effects can be massive. I know people say it all the time, but there's a reason that sleep deprivation is used as a form of torture. You can't think straight. You can't function. If I don't sleep I either get teary or clumsy (or both). Sleep helps you regulate your moods. It's highly, highly undervalued. If you're like me and craving a perfect – or just a better – night's sleep, it's really worth following the suggestions below to change your bedtime habits and make a positive difference.

- Make sure the room is dark and quiet. If you're trying to help a child to sleep and total darkness is an issue for them, having a night-light on is fine – there's no point making them stressed, as then they definitely won't sleep.

- Make sure you're not too hot or too cold.

- Make sure your bed is comfortable.

- Avoid screens. Light from tablets and computers and some e-readers can trick the body into thinking it's daylight when it's not (it's all about the circadian rhythms). If your body doesn't know night from day then it's small wonder it does its best to keep you awake when you should really be asleep, which then leaves you exhausted when you need to concentrate on work, school, or anything else. The rule in our house is no screens in bedrooms – or it was until home schooling. It's a rule that's much harder to enforce when they are working in their bedrooms. The goalposts have moved, but outside of school and homework it's still an absolute no.

- Getting out and doing some exercise during the day will help you feel tired and relaxed when it comes to bedtime.

- Create a routine in which you go to bed and get up at the same time every day (set your alarm if you need to).

- Turn your alarm clock away from the bed – clockwatching makes things worse, not better.

- For little ones afraid of monsters that come out at night, I recommend using 'monster spray' (room spray/air freshener) in cupboards and under the bed, to get rid of scary creatures. Whenever Ava smells sandalwood, she remembers me doing this.

 DON'T

- Have too much caffeine – especially in the late afternoon and evening. People typically think of coffee as the main culprit here, but tea, cola drinks and chocolate can all have the same effect. You should avoid all these for at least six hours before going to bed.

- Eat a heavy meal or do strenuous exercise too close to bedtime.

- Nap during the day.

- Work or study in the hour and a half before bed. A racing or stimulated brain won't help you drop off easily.

- Drink alcohol (one for the adults, obviously). When people talk about nightcaps it promotes the idea that alcohol can help you sleep, but actually it's the opposite and is more likely to cause broken sleep or make you wake early.

- Smoke – another one for the grown-ups. Nicotine is a stimulant, so it's the last thing that will help you when you're worried you're not getting enough sleep.

And if you can't get to sleep don't lie there stressing about it (it really won't help!). Get up, go into another room and read quietly for 30 minutes or so, then go back to bed when you start to feel sleepy. I love reading, but if I'm tired I find it really helps me to switch off and get to sleep; I find as soon as I get to the third page I can't keep my eyes open. So I make sure I always give my girls half an hour to read before bed, irrespective of what else is going on, so that they have that half an hour of chill time. It's so important to have the time and space to decompress.

HOW TO

Get a good skin routine going

If you have good skin it's easy to think you don't need to bother with a routine, but one day you'll actually be very glad you did. And if you have problem skin – be it dry, greasy, or prone to spots – a simple routine can make all the difference.

However, whatever your skin type, I have one rule above all others:

TAKE YOUR MAKE-UP OFF!

It's never too early to get into good habits, and a bit of self-care is always a good thing. Although these days my own routine is really quite basic, I think back to my teens when I had loads of different products and I don't want to take that fun away from them.

Now my girls are forming their own skincare routines. I look at what they have out on their sink – enough to fill a Boots counter, with everything from unicorn bath bombs through to lotions and potions – but as long as it's not ruining their skin, I'm happy with them experimenting and enjoying it. They just need to know that if they do put on a bit of make-up they have to remove it or it will block or clog their pores.

You don't have to fill your bathroom or dressing table with loads of different creams and products to take good care of your skin, just get yourself into a routine and repeat it in the morning and just before you go to bed. If you're not sure where to start, here's a guide to the basics.

Cleanse

Basically, this does what it says on the tin; it's effectively washing your face with a product that's kinder to your skin than soap and water and that gets rid of the dirt that clogs your pores. Finding the right cleanser is important. It doesn't have to be expensive but it does have to be one that suits your skin. If your skin is greasy, for example, you don't want one that's oily; if it's sensitive you'll want one that doesn't contain potential irritants such as perfume or alcohol, and so on. So get to know your skin and get the right products for it.

Tone

This is basically all about rebalancing the skin. Some toners, acids, or serums hydrate the skin, while others exfoliate. Again, what you use should be governed by your skin type. I also use an eye cream before moving to the next stage:

Moisturize

This is all about rehydrating your skin. Just as with the other products in your routine, you'll need a moisturizer that suits your skin.

SPF

As a final step in the morning, after applying moisturizer always apply sunscreen with a SPF of at least 30, to keep your skin healthy and protected from sun damage. If you get your kids into the routine of applying SPF now, you'll set them up with good habits for the rest of their life.

Continued overleaf →

Here are a few top tips that I have shared with my girls about looking after their skin:

- Never share make-up with your friends! Hygiene is really important. I've worked with countless make-up artists and they clean and resharpen everything in between different clients and jobs. I was on set once when a less-experienced assistant got into trouble for using the same sponge to dab down all the different models. Not good!

- If you drop a brush onto the floor, clean it before using it again (would you smear your face all over the floor? No!). When it comes to cleaning make-up brushes, the best thing to use is good old-fashioned shampoo and warm water. You can get special remover sprays and things that do it very quickly, but if you're at home this works wonders and is much cheaper!

- I'll say it again: always wear an SPF.

- Going to bed with make-up on is a cardinal sin.

Don't forget, a lot of products feed on your fears about your skin to make you buy them. 'Use this and your spots will vanish!' 'Use this and you'll look ten years younger!' So to prevent yourself falling for the hype, I think it's important to have to have a very clear idea about what creams are there to do, as opposed to thinking that they are some kind of magic potion.

You also need to remember that we all have different skins and a lot of what will work for you is down to your ethnicity, your skin type, your background, your age and so many other components – including cold weather, hot weather, hormones and more. I've got girlfriends who are Black and they live by their moisturizer; I didn't realize that without it your skin can look quite grey and sallow. The important thing is to find out what works for YOU.

IS EXPENSIVE ALWAYS BETTER?

No! Having worked in the creation of brands and understanding what goes into them, I've learned that using what works with your skin is the most important thing. If you throw more money at it, it's not necessarily going to give you better results. With expensive brands so much of the money goes into the packaging and the marketing.

If you are paying more for a cream understand what the components are. I learned when I was producing make-up myself that one of the High-Street brands was coming out of the same factory as one of the very top brands, so understanding what you are getting for your money really matters.

HOW TO

Keep plaits pristine overnight

Most mornings there's no way I have time to do the girls' hair for school in between making sure everyone is up, dressed, teeth brushed, piano practice done, baby fed, and all while getting myself ready for work. So I have found that the trick is to do whatever plaits they're after the night before – especially on blended family days when there are three of them to do in a row.

But how do you make sure the style stays pristine overnight? Simple – you just need the tights trick.

1   Plait and fasten the hair as desired.

2   Take a pair of tights and pull them down carefully over the hair.

3   Tie the legs round and fasten them in a bow at the front.

4   School hair – ready to go!

Note: While tights work brilliantly for my girls' hair, a friend, whose children have incredible afro curls, finds that they can be too harsh and swears by using a silk scarf instead. It's worth experimenting with what works best for you and your hair type.

Cope with spots

Managing acne and skin conditions that linger is something that's very close to my heart, having seen a close family member really suffer with their skin. And I say suffer because it can be hugely debilitating and affect people's confidence massively.

Everyone gets the odd spot or outbreak. It might be down to hormones (period spots, anyone?) or all manner of other things, but this is very different from having acne or other severe skin problems that are continuous.

FOR EVERYDAY PROBLEMS

- A good skincare routine (see page 20) is extra important if you are prone to breakouts or spots.

- Never squeeze spots. I know it's tempting, but it can cause scarring or infection. The more you touch your spot, the more dirt you bring to the affected area and the worse you'll make it.

- Flare-ups won't disappear overnight, but it's important to always use the right products to help with spots or blemishes. Don't resort to applying 'homemade' treatments such as surgical spirit, toothpaste or perfume to the spot. (Yes, I tried this in the hope it would dry the spot out. It didn't, it just lingered and looked red and angry!) Do your research and find a product that works but won't damage your skin long term.

WHEN TO SEE A DOCTOR

Acne is something that you need professional, clinical help to deal with. It's not a case of throwing products at your skin; it requires an understanding of what your hormones are doing (teenage acne often goes hand in hand with very heavy periods and even hair loss) and you might need professional advice to find the cause and corresponding treatment.

The investigations can be difficult and the treatment can take time to get right. It's a tough journey; it can knock your confidence and require courage to do things that would be otherwise quite normal, such as going to school, but it's worth the effort in order to solve the problem and not create new issues for the future.

If it's a young person who's going through it, it's essential to learn how to discuss their skin and how they feel about it without making them feel worse. Of course there is more to someone than their skin, but when you are a teenager how you look is so important. So, acknowledge how hard it is and make time and space for them to have a cry, but don't let it take over their lives. The most important thing to do if you think you or your child has a problem is to visit your doctor, get it diagnosed properly, and get the help you really need.

If you know someone suffering with acne ...

- Think before you speak. I truly cannot believe how insensitive some people can be. It's not something to joke about or make personal comments about. If in doubt, say nothing.

- Understand that the person will be only too aware of their condition. You won't be the first to notice it! It's also probable that they will be doing everything possible to treat it. It takes time.

- Don't suggest trying this, that, and the other if they haven't asked your advice. If someone is receiving proper medical treatment they will already be using the best things to treat their skin type and issue.

- Don't tell someone that they should stop putting make-up on their skin. Often sufferers wear make-up to cover the spots and give themselves the confidence to face other people.

Remove unwanted body hair

Some women are happy to let their body hair grow and flow, others prefer to get rid of the lot – and then there's pretty much everything in between.

The decision about how much hair to remove, if any, and where from can also vary enormously; different people (and cultures) can have very different views on this. I remember when Julia Roberts didn't shave her armpits and it was front-page news in the UK. In many other European countries that would have been so confusing, with everyone wondering what all the fuss was about.

We've been really open about it in our household. Even before Ava hit puberty, this was something we started to talk about. I've told the girls, this is what society says, this is what you can do, and this is how some people treat it – I've even shown them photos where people dye their body hair pink and highlight it! I don't agree with telling them it has to be a certain way. I have friends whose mothers told them they had to lose weight, or remove hair, or cut their hair, or change what they were wearing when they were kids, and there comes a point when you're projecting so much of yourself and your beliefs onto your child that you're not really teaching them to think for themselves. They may well have different views from me, and that's not a problem.

The girls know they need to figure out what works for them and I will help them get to grips with whatever method they choose. I remember all too well not being allowed to shave my legs as a teenager. I was determined to do it anyway, so locked the bathroom door, took my dad's cut-throat razor, and attempted to do it dry. So many cuts! I didn't have a clue. So it's probably no great surprise that my view is that they're going to do it anyway, so they should be shown how to do it properly and safely.

I find it fascinating how differently men and women approach shaving. For boys it is a rite of passage that's almost celebratory, whereas for girls it's hush-hush and seems shrouded in shame. I didn't want that for my girls so it was important to me to approach it in an open and light-hearted way. So I've said to them, look here's the deal. There are the various things you can do to get rid of excess hair if it makes you feel uncomfortable, and it's your choice and no one else's, but I do think it's really important to present all the options:

TWEEZING: Good for eyebrows or those stray facial hairs that appear from nowhere when you reach a certain age. (I remember clearly how my granny used to have a few hairs on her chin and I was fascinated by them as a child!) Tweezers are not so good for large areas – though I do wonder how long it would take to do one leg …

THREADING: A simple strand of cotton turns out to be a suprisingly useful opponent when up against unwanted hair. It traps, pulls, and removes in the same way as tweezers and is brilliant for eyebrows – if you know what you are doing! If you don't, you may end up losing the lot, so this is definitely one that's best left in the hands of the experts.

CREAMS: The most off-putting thing about these was always the smell, which could almost strip the lining of your nostrils if you got too close. But that's vastly improved these days, making this a good, economical, and pain-free option. It's great for those just starting out on hair removal for all those reasons – and the fact that it doesn't involve sharp blades. The downsides are that you'll need to do it fairly regularly and it can get messy. You should also avoid using it on facial hair. Always follow the instructions on the packaging, and do a test patch before starting on a large area, to check for skin sensitivity.

EPILATORS: Effective but not for the faint-hearted. If we are giving the various methods a fear-factor score, this is right up there. I've got loads of friends who swear by it but it can hurt! These are useful if you have sensitive skin or are on a certain medication that doesn't allow the use of cream or waxing. There are lots of different models on the market – some for dry use and some for wet – but they all work in much the same way, with either tweezer heads or rotating blades to lift and remove hair from the root. They can come with different attachments for different areas and the results can be excellent and long-lasting.

WAXING: Another solution that follows the no-pain, no-gain philosophy. It's quick, it works well, but it's also fair to say that it smarts a bit (which is a bit of an understatement depending on what and where on your body you do this). No one told me that if you take a pain killer half an hour before you're going to have a much better time of it. I could really have done with that information! You can do it yourself with a kit or lie back and think of England while a professional does it for you. The upside is that it will help to slow future hair growth; the downside is that you may end up with the odd ingrowing hair.

IPL OR LASER: Considerably more expensive but this technique can permanently reduce regrowth after a number of regular sessions. I'm not very hairy anyway but because I model bikinis, this is what I went for. That said, I wouldn't allow my daughters to go anywhere near a laser until they are over 18.

Take pride in your appearance

There can be a fine line between making the best of yourself and becoming vain or self-obsessed. On the one hand it's good to think 'people should take me as I am', but if you have a job to do in a professional capacity alongside other people and clients, you need to be dressed appropriately.

I believe that if you put yourself together well, you are essentially saying that you have pride in who you are and it helps you to get yourself into a positive mindset. It's like when I tell the girls not to leave their bedrooms in a state because it sets the tone for the rest of the day. For me, if you can make your bed, if you can have a proper breakfast, if you can get out of the house on time, if you can do your schoolwork … all these tiny little hurdles mean you've got your brain in some kind of order that will make you feel organized and together.

Of course I want my girls to feel they look nice, and we talk about this, but I also don't want them to obsess about it. That balance is important and it has to come from me as an example.

MY GOLDEN RULES FOR PERSONAL APPEARANCE ARE:

• Being clean and tidy matters. It will always help you feel better about yourself.

• Be proud of who you are, enjoy being a woman, and make the best of yourself, but don't place all your value on your appearance. I say to the girls that they need to be able to sell themselves on their personality and what they have to offer and not just on their appearance. Imagine being interviewed over the phone where they can't see your great make-up or you fluttering your eyelashes or flicking your hair – all these things that the patriarchy has fed to us for so long, telling us that we are all in competition for the scraps they decide to give us. This is where we make the changes.

These are the top ones, but there are other rules that I add to this that are for my girls:

1   I never let my friends talk or worry about their own weight or anyone else's in front of my kids.

2   I make sure my kids don't see me looking at myself in the mirror in a negative way – even when I was how many stone heavier after having the baby.

3   I show them that I'm celebrating my body. There are some things, trust me, that go against how I might be feeling at the time, but I know that my girls will benefit from seeing me accept these as part and parcel of who I am, as opposed to me talking badly about myself because of them. The best thing about this is that it stops me wallowing, too.

4   I encourage them to help me get ready by asking them what they think will go with this or that, and to enjoy looking at colour blocking with me and what works or looks good together. We also have good chats about fashion and how it changes across history. Fashion and looks are often historically, politically, and socially related. Today women feel emancipated and more free to celebrate themselves. Anything goes.

In the roaring Twenties women couldn't wait to lop off their hair in an act of rebellion, fighting against the social constraints of what was deemed *feminine* pre-war. In the Thirties trousers were worn after Coco Chanel liberated women from corsets and dresses. The Fifties saw Marylin Monroe bring curves back into fashion, whereas the introduction of birth control and the sexual revolution of the Sixties meant miniskirts ruled and figures became more slight. The Eighties brought the 'supermodels' (Cindy Crawford and her gang of Amazonian women), in full make-up and colour, and then the Nineties introduced the waif. When I was a teen, Kate Moss was the poster girl for being super slim. Today it seems to be about curvy bottoms and big hips. It's a lot to keep up with! I love where we are at now. Everything feels more accepting and celebratory. History might go in fads, but ultimately you are what you are and you need to make the best of it.

So, while I think appearance matters, I'll say again that it is about balance. Worrying constantly about the way we look can make it feel as though we only value ourselves on that basis, so we need to remind ourselves that we are also valued for the attributes we can work on – such as being funny, kind, smart, hardworking, sporty. It's a valuable life lesson at any age.

HOW TO

Avoid bad breath

Let's face it, nobody wants to be that person who's got halitosis or things stuck in their teeth. You'd like to think a friend would let you know if there's a problem, but it's never quite that simple.

WHAT CAUSES BAD BREATH?

Lots of things, including eating spicy or strong-smelling foods, such as garlic, onions, curry, smoking, but also various medical conditions and dental problems.

HOW DO YOU KNOW IF YOU HAVE BAD BREATH?

Obviously if people recoil every time you go near them it's going to be a pretty clear sign, but otherwise it can be quite hard to tell. There are a few things you can try.

- Ask someone you're close to for their honest opinion – even if you don't like the answer, it's better to know.

- Breathe into your cupped hands and see how it smells. This is probably not as accurate a method as the above, but it's worth a go.

- Lick your wrist, give it a moment or two to dry and then sniff it. No, I'd never heard of this before either, but apparently it is a legitimate test and I know more than one person who's grown up doing this and they swear by it.

- Use floss between your back teeth and then smell it.

WHAT CAN YOU DO ABOUT IT?

The most important thing to do is maintain great dental hygiene, which is a really valuable life skill in itself. Kids will be the first to skip brushing their teeth, so it's a good idea to get them to understand how important it is and why it matters. Even sticking to the basics really helps in keeping bad breath at bay:

- Brush your teeth for at least two minutes twice a day (and don't rinse with water afterwards).

- Floss regularly.

- Make sure you use a fluoride toothpaste.

- Don't eat too much sugar.

- Get regular dental check-ups.

Oh, and top life rule – if somebody offers you a mint, never say no.

Stop blonde hair going green in a swimming pool

The combination of blonde hair and swimming pools is not always a good one. I know because I've been there; over the years I've dyed my hair all sorts of colours and learned the hard way that a quick dip can leave your locks with an unappealing greenish tinge –somewhere between overboiled cabbage and radioactive lettuce. It's not a great look.

HOW CAN YOU STOP IT HAPPENING?
Wet your hair with clean water before you go for a dip. Hair strands are super-porous so they'll absorb whatever you pour onto them before you get in the pool. Anything after that (the pool water) is mainly surplus. You can also use a bit of conditioner to help create a waterproof barrier.

TOO LATE – I LOOK LIKE KERMIT
Don't panic – there are a few things you can do to get safely back to blonde. You can buy various shampoos and treatments specially formulated to remove the brassiness by getting rid of the chlorine, salts, and minerals that cause the problem. Or you can raid the kitchen cupboards and use tomato ketchup/purée, which will help balance the pH levels and correct the colour. However, do note that it does go an awful scary red shade at first – but once you wash it it will be absolutely fine!

2

A friend in need

Saying sorry.
Ava, aged 7, after her
first shop breakage.

Working mum.
Know your limits ...
the juggle is real

Sisters and friends. Keep close to those who love you. Ava, aged 9, and Hero, aged 6

Say sorry

**Elton John wasn't wrong when he said that sorry seems to be
the hardest word. Apologizing – and sounding like you mean it
– can take guts, but it's an important thing to be able to do.
I come from the era when children were never apologized to,
so I don't remember my parents ever saying sorry to me.
And as a result I think I've really had to speak to myself and
tell myself that I need to admit it when I've made a mistake,
and I make a point of doing this with everyone,
but most importantly with the children.**

I've often said to them, I'm going to hold my hands up and say sorry to you, and the reason
I do that is that I don't want them to think that just because I'm an adult I always get things
right. Adults get it wrong a lot and it's important to learn that everybody makes mistakes –
but not everyone can easily say sorry and it's an important skill to learn. I've told them that
the mark of a strong woman is actually owning up when things go wrong. It's so easy to take
the accolades when things go right, but if you're prepared to take those then you also need
to take responsibility when things go wrong. I make a point of showing them this myself, so
they can see how I deal with it, too.

*'Adults get it wrong a lot and it's important
to learn that everybody makes mistakes.'*

WHEN IT'S GOOD TO SAY SORRY

There's a very British habit of apologizing when it really isn't necessary (such as when someone bumps into you. Their fault!), but that said, it's always good to recognize when is the right time to say sorry. So, if you need reminding (as we all do now and then) these are always good reasons to apologize:

- Because you were wrong.

- Because you purposely did or said something that upset someone else.

- Because you inadvertently did or said something that upset someone else.

- Because you acted in your own self-interest and didn't think about others.

- Because you broke something.

- Because you forgot something.

- Because you ate the last biscuit.

HOW TO SAY SORRY LIKE YOU MEAN IT

A half-hearted, insincere, or grudging apology can be worse than no apology at all. So, here's how to say sorry – and mean it.

ALWAYS include the words 'I'm sorry' or 'I apologize'

NEVER follow those with 'but ...'

TRY TO acknowledge what you did wrong – it will show that you have really taken on board what you did or didn't do, and that your apology is genuine, and give the reason why you're apologizing. It's too easy to just say sorry without saying what you're sorry for.

The best way to prove your apology is genuine is by showing that you have learned from it and by not doing/saying the thing that's led to you having to say sorry again. If I've said something that hurts my children's feelings, or I've overreacted to something they've done, I make a point of showing them that I am sorry by doing things differently next time round. But I expect the same from them, they know that sorry looks like not doing the same thing again. It's become a bit of a running joke in our house; they'll say 'I'll shoooooowwww you I'm sorry', but it works, and we all stick to it.

Know when to keep a secret

'Can you keep a secret?'

'I'll tell you if you promise not to tell anyone else ...'

How many times have we all heard these words? We've all been in situations where we think we can trust someone, but that's the thing about secrets. You might tell just one person then they will tell one person, and they will tell one person ('only one'), and suddenly it's not such a secret anymore. This is as true in the world of celebrity as it is in the playground or any workplace.

Secrets can almost galvanize a friendship – 'I'm going to show you how special you are to me by letting you in on this information'. Sometimes they are a test of a friendship, to see if you keep the secret or spill the beans to someone else as just some gossip. Some of us are definitely better at keeping secrets than others, but whatever you're like, you definitely do NOT want to be that person who everyone knows as the one who can't keep a secret to save their life.

That said, there are different kinds of secrets. Some are absolutely for keeping:

- 'I've got an amazing new job/book deal/role but I have to keep shtum about it until it's formally announced ...'

- 'We are throwing a surprise party for ...'

- 'I'm getting this for her birthday but don't tell her ...'

You don't want to ruin a great surprise that people have put time, effort, and thought into.

You don't want to leak information that's been shared with you and lessen the impact of a big announcement.

You don't want to let slip that someone is going to get the gift they have longed for.

But other secrets can be less straightforward. It can be difficult to know whether to keep them to yourself or not – either because you are concerned about the person the secret is about or because the stress of holding that knowledge can be too heavy a burden.

Times you should *not* keep a secret include:

- When someone could be in danger

- When someone might cause harm to another person

- When it is making you worried or anxious.

In these circumstances it's important to share your concerns with someone you can trust and who will be able to help work out a constructive course of action.

TEACHING YOUR KIDS ABOUT SECRETS

I tell my girls that they should always keep a secret unless there's a Bat sign shining up in the sky as an indication that they really need to do something, and then it might be time for parents to step in and deal with it – for instance, when someone's welfare is at risk or keeping the secret can effectively amount to lying and get them into trouble. It's really important to have an open dialogue with your children so that they know they can trust you if there's something that they feel they shouldn't be keeping to themselves. If this happens:

1   Let them know that you won't break the secret unless it is absolutely necessary. Mine have come to me with all sorts of things, some of which have been really tricky. Friends in real trouble with other friends, bullies, online situations, people getting divorced and complications thereof, potential harm, eating disorders, dark thoughts … Children also need to know that some adults misuse the word 'secret' to abuse their own position and that is when a secret must never be kept. If it feels wrong, it is wrong.

2   If you do feel you need to take it further, keep them in the loop. When one of my children talked to me about how a friend was being treated by a family member I explained I was going to deal with it and that they should trust me to do it properly, but it was too big a secret for me and certainly too big for her, so I brought in extra professional help.

3   They will – of course – worry that letting you in on a secret they have promised not to share is going to backfire on them – with you, another adult, or the person it concerns. When there was an issue at school, I made it very clear to the teacher that it couldn't have any implications for my daughter as otherwise they'd be taking two children down. They were great about it and things were better all round as a result. A definite win.

Be persuasive

It's all about hustling. Whether it's just trying to get closer to the school gate through a throng of chatting parents when you're in a rush/late, or asking for a coffee when the shop's about to close, I love the hustle that trying to get people onside can bring.

The important things to remember are:

- Be polite – you'll get nowhere if you are rude. I've stepped in many times when I have heard people being unacceptably rude.

- Be confident – but not entitled.

- Know when it's appropriate to be cheeky or funny, helpful or apologetic.

- Know when to shut up, back down, and let it go.

We were at the park and my stepdaughter dropped her ice cream. She hadn't even had one taste of it when it ended up on the floor and she was just resigned to the fact that that was that. I told her 'No. Go back to the ice-cream van and explain what's happened and see if he'll replace it.' She said, 'I can't, because it was my fault. I dropped it.' I acknowledged that she was right, but I convinced her it was still worth trying. If she didn't get another ice cream, no problem, she was no worse off – but she might just get another one so there was nothing to lose. I said, 'Just explain that we bought seven ice creams, I dropped mine, it was an awful accident, I take complete and utter responsibility for it. But if you could find it in your heart just to give me another ice cream, I'd be so grateful.' She came back with an ice cream and it was like she'd won the lottery. And it was a great lesson for her.

Ultimately, if you demand something from someone it's likely not going to happen, but if you offer a polite and reasonable resolution, or help problem-solve, you'll be amazed how often you will be rewarded for that.

Be a good listener

We all need a friendly ear at times – and it's great to be able to offer the same in return. It's good to know that you are someone people feel they can turn to, but if that is the case, it's important to listen in a way that will really make a difference.

'If someone wants to share a problem or talk about something that's worrying them, let them talk. Don't jump in and try to fix things straight away – sometimes there are solutions you can help with, but those can come later.'

Often people just need to offload without interruption. I learned this lesson when I was around 22. We were listening to a friend moaning about breaking up with his boyfriend for ages and we were all chipping in with, 'Have you tried this? Have you done this? You could try this that and the other...' Then another guy in the room just turned round and said, 'Just let him vent'. It hadn't occurred to me that all he wanted to do was to rant and be listened to; it was like an epiphany. I thought, 'Of course. He doesn't want us to fix this. He just wants to be able to get it all out.'

If you are worried that you are seeming not engaged in the conversation if you're not speaking, you can show the other person that you are really listening by making the right noises. I find asking 'How did that make you feel?' or agreeing, 'Yes, that sounds awful' can not only show a bit of solidarity but also allow people to continue talking without worrying that they are taking up too much of your time, or that you've stopped listening.

Mostly people just want to be heard, but if they do want suggestions of how to deal with a situation they will ask for them. It's like when your child comes home raging because one of their friends has got a new friend. All you can do is listen, sympathize, and be there. The chances are it will all resolve itself pretty quickly anyway. There are times when we all need a cheerleader or someone to walk through the fire with us. When I suffered my miscarriages, I would call my friends and cry down the phone, or not be able to say a word, but my friends would listen to my sobs and silence, knowing that I just needed someone to say 'It's okay'.

Make conversation

For some people, making small talk comes naturally. For others it's like pulling teeth and requires a lot of effort. But if the very thought of having to fill awkward silences fills you with dread, worry not: conversation is a skill you can learn and the principles will see you through pretty much any social occasion.

These are my tips learned from years of formal and informal situations:

- Don't just talk about yourself. A lot of people do this when they get nervous but the best way to make conversation is to ask the other person/people about themselves. They will remember you for it.

- You can talk about really simple stuff: What have you been doing today? What are your plans? Often the most dull-seeming questions can lead to the most exciting conversations.

Listen, really listen, when the other person tells you something. It's nice to be able to react to it.

- Try not to give one-word answers – if someone asks 'How are you?', replying 'Fine' will close down the conversation rather than opening it up. Instead, say something like, 'I'm really well, thank you. How are you?' Respond, then ask a question back.

- Make eye contact – that's a life skill in its own right. If you walk into a room and just hide in the corner no one will even know you're there. So to get what you want – whether it's being served at the bar, meeting someone, finding out where the loo is, or making conversation – you can't be invisible. Walk into the room, have a look around, be curious.

Making conversation is something we practise a lot in our house – and Hero's an absolute gem at it. She's got phenomenal observational skills, so she might start a conversation with someone saying, 'I love your earrings. Where did you get them from?' and then, 'Who's your favourite drag queen?' You never quite know what's coming from her.

'I find it's often easiest to chat over dinner when we're all together, and I will always ask 'How was your day? What did you get up to today?' It's the perfect start. It's about showing interest – and that can mean a lot to people.'

Weirdly, there are some old-fashioned rules about what you shouldn't discuss and I stand by them – religion, politics, and finances. It's one thing making conversation, it's another upsetting, offending, or intimidating someone with your chat.

Get out of a conversation

Having found myself, at various points over the years, in a position where extricating myself from a conversation is definitely the best way forward, I've made sure that this is something we practise a lot too! I'm aware that I take my girls to places where they might find themselves in a position of not always wanting to listen to the adult conversations around them, so I've armed them with conversational skills, but equally with an understanding of the directions they don't need to go in, and how to avoid them, as well.

1   If you're not comfortable in a conversation, find a way to get out of it.

2   A simple 'Please excuse me', or 'Excuse me, I just need to go and speak to my mum' can work wonders.

3   Another way to exit a conversation politely is to say 'I'm so sorry, I've just remembered something I need to go and do'.

4   Don't ever feel you need to talk about things that make you uncomfortable. We've discussed the fact that there are some things you don't ever speak about and one of them is money. So when someone recently asked Ava how much she was making from her piano teaching, she had a classic line at the ready: 'A lady never discusses her finances'. It made everyone laugh, but it also got her out of an awkward situation quickly and with good humour. She didn't have to reveal the amount she earned and no one was made to feel uncomfortable. It was a really good lesson in avoiding a question with charm and dignity.

5   If someone brings up a subject you don't feel happy with, there is never any shame in being honest. It can take a lot of guts to say 'I don't feel comfortable talking about this', but it's something you'd hope most people will respect.

Deal with frenemies and bullies

What is a frenemy? It's a ridiculous word, but it's a very real problem. Essentially, a frenemy is someone who can be really friendly to you to your face, but behind your back, or under every comment, there's an undercurrent of dislike or jealousy.

As Bridget Jones says, talking to a frenemy 'is like … being stung repeatedly by an enormous jellyfish.' A frenemy might say something with a smile, but it is designed to hurt. For instance: 'I love what you've done with your hair. I wouldn't have gone with that haircut personally, but you carry it well, for someone who's got a round face.' You know the kind of thing. Veiled or backhanded compliments from people who don't make you feel good about yourself at all.

HOW TO DEAL WITH THEM

Sometimes people behave like this because they feel threatened or jealous; sometimes they just get a kick out of being mean; and sometimes they behave like this with specific people or they are like this with everyone.

But there is a big difference between someone who's well-meaning but tactless and a person who is setting out to hurt you intentionally – aka, a frenemy.

1   Don't show them you are upset. I've said to the girls that if you want to go to the loo and cry, then phone me, fine. But don't let them see that they have hurt you. And it's a terrible thing that you have to say that, but it is a great life skill to learn that if you crumble on the spot, everything crumbles around you.

2   Get help. Times are changing. You don't have to put up with anyone's behaviour or bullying. Call it out if you can. And if you can't do this on your own (which is very hard to do), find allies to help and support you to tell someone. Don't put up with it alone.

Continued overleaf →

3 Don't try to make them your friend. They are not worth it and a true friend is not someone who gets a kick out of making you feel bad. Walk away with your head held high.

4 Understand that sometimes people are just silly, and they don't mean to be nasty with it. They're saying this stuff without realizing that they are putting their foot in it. But if someone starts a sentence with 'I don't mean to be rude, but ...' or 'I'm not being funny but ...' it's generally a sign that they are about to be mean. It's like a big flashing light. Likewise, 'I'm just being honest' or 'It's just my opinion' are definite warning signals. Most of the time no one has asked for their thoughts!

HOW TO ... RECOGNIZE A BULLY

Bullying takes many forms, from the more obvious – insults, intimidation, physical stuff – to gaslighting and coercion. Sometimes you won't realize you are being bullied by someone until you've been out of that friendship or relationship for a while.

Bullies come in all shapes and sizes but essentially they are people who intentionally go out of their way to make you feel bad, perhaps by saying nasty things or making comments that they know are going to upset you. Physical bullying can take many different forms, but verbal bullying can also be very damaging. The old saying 'Sticks and stones may break my bones but words will never hurt me' is something I absolutely disagree with. I've been there and it's really tough.

Bullies can also sadly be in your family. By this, I mean the people who are meant to love you, but who make things impossible for you. It is not okay for anyone, family or friend, to mistreat you. Some people are bullied because of their sexuality, job, partner, race ... or for just being around. For those that find themselves in toxic family set-ups, relationships, or friendships, this is not okay. No one should control or belittle you. Ever.

People's words can resonate and rattle around in your brain for the rest of your life if you let them. Most adults can remember exactly who was horrible to them at school – even if it's decades later. I certainly can. I remember one of them telling me the nit nurse was coming in and making me take my hair out. It was school photo day and there was no nit nurse and I just had really terrible hair in the pictures. So having been there and experienced these sorts of behaviours, as a child and as an adult, it's really important to me that I give the girls the tools to cope if they face similar situations.

HOW TO … DEAL WITH BULLIES

1   Again, it's about not letting them see how much they have hurt you. If they take pleasure in upsetting you, then if they can see it's working, they will come back for more. Try to show you are not afraid – even if you are inside.

2   Try to keep your head as strong as your heart and body. Finding the strength to throw those hurtful words away will pay dividends. Imagine a bin on a computer: put them in there and then press empty. Gone. I wish I had learned this earlier, it would have saved me a lot of heartache.

3   Remember that bullies are simply demonstrating how NOT to behave. If you can, when someone is being unkind, show them that you're standing your ground. This can be tough. But also know when to walk away with your head held high; if the bullying turns physical, you're outnumbered, or if you're concerned for your well-being, it's important to get away to a place of safety as quickly as possible.

DEALING WITH ONLINE ABUSE

Social media bullying can be harder to escape simply because of the scale and the way that things can spread like wildfire, but as with any fire, it's best to tackle it before it spreads or gets out of control. It can be tempting to respond impulsively, but this can do more harm than good, as whatever you post will be out there forever – even if you decide to delete the words afterwards, there's a chance someone will already have screenshotted it.

That said, screenshotting can be useful; if you are bullied on social media, take a copy to keep as evidence; it's easy for bullies to delete and deny and this stops them being able to do that. And don't try to deal with it alone – instead talk to a parent, a teacher, or another trusted adult.

3

Let's talk about...

Having a voice and knowing how to use it.
Ava, aged 8

with an NGO delivering
a fridge to a hospital in
Nepal. Use your voice to
empower others

Teaching
rescued
child brides
in Tanzania
with Save
the Children

Ava, aged 8, and Hero, aged 5, on set, learning about
the working environment

Schoolgirls braiding my hair,
with Save the Children

Hero, aged 5 and Ava, aged 8,
in Filipina national dress

Ava, aged 14, standing up to
racism and homophobia

Dear Ava,

Your mum told us about how you left a friend's house last weekend because her brother (and his friends) were making racist & homophobic comments. You're probably a bit embarrassed for being praised for doing this, but it is worth saying how important – and impressive – this is. It's impressive because I know grown adults that wouldn't have the courage to do this. Even at their age, they're still held back from challenging people's bigoted views because they are worried how others will respond.

It's important because your actions can, and will, have an impact on other people – not just what they think, but also what they do and say in the future. People say bigoted things for lots of reasons. For some it's repeating the messages they heard growing up, for others they're too intellectually-lazy to consider another opinion and for some, they just

want a cheap laugh. But words are important. Depressingly, LGBTQ+ teenagers are five times more likely to take their own life than other people their own age. And mental health issues including depression & anxiety are far greater in black communities than others. Sadly, stats like this are all too common across communities in the UK, from people with disabilities to those that come from economically disadvantaged (ie poorer) households.

Whilst people may say "I'm only joking", these negative everyday interactions are often what leads to these terrible outcomes. It's the racist joke in the classroom, the homophobic taunt thrown into a heated argument or the sharing of someone's background on a social media post that can – and does – have a huge impact on people. Hopefully you will have encouraged those people

to consider the impact of their words & develop more mature thinking. At the very least, you may have made them think twice before they say anything racist or homophobic in future. And if that means someone hears one less negative comment about who they are, that is a wonderful thing.

We are very proud of you.

Lots of Love,

The Uncles x

Talk about racism

Growing up mixed race in Norfolk in the 1980s wasn't always easy. To the Filipino community I wasn't Filipina, to the white community I wasn't white. I'd get asked if I was Chinese or Thai. It was hard to define who I was. And then there's the fact that mixed-race people so often get lumped together in one mixed-race pot, even though our ethnicities and backgrounds might be poles apart.

I'm also very aware that what I went through in my childhood might be completely different to what other mixed-race and Black friends might have experienced, and I tell my children never to match their story with anyone else's. If someone shares their experience with you, you don't need to jump in with yours – you haven't walked in their shoes.

You should also consider that things can appear very different to those on the inside: there are stories and situations that people will tell me about that I find hilarious because they chime with my own heritage, for example, but I'm not sure that other friends get them at all.

Racism is, of course, a huge and complex subject. But when it comes to talking about it, these are some of the things I feel are hugely important to share with other people, and in particular my children:

1   **Listen**. If, for example, a Black man is telling his story then you can't identify with it fully if you are not a Black man because it's not your story. Listen and learn.

2   **Be respectful**. If someone tells you their name and it's unfamiliar to you, learn it and pronounce it properly. Don't oversimplify it for your own ease; if you are unsure, far better to ask, respectfully, for clarification. Never, ever make a joke of it being 'complicated' or 'weird'.

3   **Educate yourself**. This is the most important thing you can do. It is not the job of people from different races to educate you. You must do this for yourself. Find out about the different religious holidays and how they are marked or celebrated. Understand what is and isn't appropriate in terms of religious and cultural customs for other people.

Encourage your kids to ask questions and explore. Ava recently took a brave stand and left a party when racist and homophobic comments were made. When she pointed out how inappropriate these were, her protest was dismissed: 'We're just joking', followed by 'I'm not racist. I actually have loads of Black friends'. Being in the proximity of people of colour doesn't make you any less racist, just as standing next to a woman doesn't make you less sexist.

4   **Beware casual racism**. It might be meant as a compliment rather than a dig, but avoid saying things like, 'Oh, lucky you, never having to get a tan'. If you're on the receiving end it doesn't feel great. A lot of the slurs I experienced when I was younger came from pure ignorance, even though I didn't necessarily understand that at the time. People would ask if I came to their house would I be able to use a knife and fork, or did I need chopsticks? They'd say I was lucky because I could tan easily. On social media, I recently called out a woman who said I'd had my lips done, but I have the same lips as my Filipino ancestors. Ignorance never makes this right; if you are on the receiving end of these comments, it's worth explaining why this wasn't an appropriate thing to say. It's not always easy to do and it can be so awkward, but it will stop people perpetuating these mistakes and having more awkward situations.

5   **Avoid cultural appropriation**. This is a trend that's pretty rife at the moment, and includes things like wearing other people's traditional dress (or hairstyles) as a fashion statement, using sacred objects or symbols in an off-hand or jokey way, or speaking on behalf of a group of which you are not a part. This came up in our house recently – the question was: How many plaits can you have before they become cornrows? Are they culturally appropriate?

The plaits themselves are not the problem; it's what accompanies them. Are you wearing them and pretending to be something you're not? And as a result, are you benefitting or gaining privilege and advantage by passing yourself off as another race without knowing, living, and understanding the rest of the history? When I attended an Indian wedding, my friend's family painted mendhi/henna onto my hands. They included me and shared their culture. In return, I was respectful and grateful. The line between what's acceptable and what really isn't can sometimes be a fine one, so never assume and don't be frightened to ask the question. Wanting to understand and explore other cultures is great, but it should be done in the right way and with respect. It's too easy to get it VERY wrong. You can't run Black Awareness Month without a Black person in the room, and you can't speak for women if there isn't a woman alongside you, either.

Continued overleaf →

6   **Don't make excuses for people**. Times have changed and what might have been acceptable once often – rightly – isn't any more. No one should be made to feel uncomfortable. Flippant remarks that are racist or anti-Semitic or homophobic should never be tolerated, even if they are intended in jest (there's never anything funny about racism) or out of a lack of understanding. It's easy to make excuses and say things like, 'Oh but they're old, they're from a different generation' when people come out with things that are offensive. Brushing it off as 'That's just how things used to be' doesn't wash. People didn't used to have phones – now everyone knows how to use them. We can't pick and choose the things that need to move on and that don't. Again, if something is no longer appropriate, even if it might have been used – albeit wrongly – without a thought in the past, it's good to explain why this is the case. It's less likely to end in an argument than just closing the conversation down with something like 'You can't say that'. And again, it will help to stop the problem being perpetuated, which is so important.

7   So often people aren't even aware that they're being racist. Yes, generally Filipinos are loving and tolerant to fault, but I don't need to hear 'My dad's nurse is a Filipina and she's lovely' or 'My cleaner is Filipino so I'm not racist'. The latter doesn't even make sense – and yet I hear variations on it often. Also, why, just because I'm Filipina, do I need to know everyone else you've ever met who comes from the Philippines?

It's important to correct casual and more explicit racism whenever it occurs, whether it comes from (or is directed at) adults or children. I've absolutely encouraged my girls to stand up to this sort of thing – although obviously without ever putting themselves in harm's way. I have heard first-hand the following shocking stereotypes: All Filipinos are such hard workers. Filipinos never complain. Filipinos work for less pay. Filipinos are used to working abroad and leaving their kids. And one of the most ignorant: 'You need a nanny? You should get a Filipina', to which I replied, 'You do know I'm Filipina?' 'Yeah, but you're different,' was the response. We no longer speak. I don't like racists!

A lovely way to get children to think more broadly and feel part of the global community is to ask them how many countries and cultures they encounter every day through the items they use or consume. Where was their T-shirt made? Their shoes? Their phone? Where did the food they ate come from? Or where did the recipe originate? What about the music they listen to? Where is the artist/singer from?

ABOVE ALL

I think it's really important to embrace and celebrate your differences; my girls have groups of Asian and Jewish friends and they enjoy exploring and learning about each other's different cultures, customs, and religious celebrations.

The most important things to remember are: always be respectful, be inclusive, and be aware.

CALLING IT OUT

I have taught my girls that racism is never acceptable and that if you want to see change you have to be the change. It can be as simple as saying 'I don't think you can say that anymore' or correcting a term that someone has used.

Someone asked me the other day, 'Why do you keep calling yourself mixed race? The term now is biracial' and I thought about it and said, 'But it's me. I can call myself what I like.' But then I thought about it again and asked myself, but should I, just because everyone else has called me that? And again, I start exploring those conversations with myself because I am of two races. But what if I was of four races? Then what do I become? So I still don't know what box I really fit into and now I am applying for nurseries for my son, it's starting all over again. Which box am I? I never know. The girls never know either. I find it infuriating that we so often find ourselves having to reduce who we are into two or three words.

The bottom line (and what I constantly reinforce with my own kids) is – if anything you hear doesn't feel right or makes you feel uncomfortable, call it out. If you see a friend of yours in that position, your own child, a sibling – if it doesn't sit well with you, even if it's not a direct hit, call it out. Allowing it to go unchecked is simply perpetuating the problem.

Talk about social media pressures

This is a tricky one for those of us who aren't digital natives; the fact that we never had to navigate the world of online one-upmanship and instant messaging in our youth means we never got the chance to learn from our own mistakes – plus there's no example set by our own parents to follow either.

In these days of smartphones, with email and various apps on tap 24/7, it can be almost impossible to escape from social media, whether it's apps we might use ourselves (Facebook, Twitter, Instagram) or those that are generally more popular with younger people (including TikTok, Snapchat, and more).

Any which way, it's absolutely something we need to get to grips with now; it's crucial to understand how all-pervasive social media can be for kids today and the issues that can cause. And while there are many great things about social media – such as connecting with friends and family who live far away, sharing tips, advice, and inspiration – there can be a darker side too: trolling, bullying, unwanted messages ...

Small wonder that most sites – such as Facebook, Bebo, Instagram, TikTok, Twitter, YouTube, House Party – say you have to be at least 13 to open an account. But – and there's always a but – there's nothing to stop kids from lying about their age and many feel pressured into having accounts like their friends once they start secondary school (if not before).

Before, gossip happened as a chat in the school toilets, but now it's all online, often with pictures, too (everyone has a smartphone and a camera to hand), so it's on a different scale altogether. All this means younger kids inevitably pick up things from their older siblings. Hero came home from school asking what some words meant that she'd heard. They were racy, but children don't have the attached emotions or context for these things like adults do. To them, they are literally just words. Don't shy away in embarrassment or they'll get their (often incorrect) information somewhere else, or learn that these are subjects to be ashamed of. It's always best if it comes from you. Tempting though it often is not to get into these things, it's really important to discuss them and to help your kids to learn from them.

And that's the thing: it's always better to know what your children are up to than to stick your head in the sand and pretend none of this is happening, even if it does lead to some difficult or awkward conversations.

1 **Educate yourself**. Social media is an ever-changing landscape (whatever did happen to Vine and Google+?). Even if you think you're fairly tech-savvy, you still need to familiarize yourself with the sites your kids might be visiting and the terminology they might be using – particularly if it's designed to throw parents off the scent (POS anyone? Parent Over Shoulder).

2 **Keep the lines of communication open – and talk with them about what they are seeing and doing.** It's so important to be open, to avoid judging, if you want to keep communicating honestly. As a parent I'm aware how easy it can be to find myself in an echo chamber on social media, and to be lulled into the idea that everyone is thinking much the same way as I do. But the echo chambers our children can find themselves in might be very different, and we need to be aware of that. What are the views they are seeing and hearing, and how do they feel about them? Making time to discuss this is key.

3 **Make it relevant**. I've shown my girls what people they relate to – generally younger people in their twenties – are doing online and the mistakes they might have made (such as making ill-advised comments that have then gone viral and they've had to retract and apologize for), and then we talk about them and what has happened as a result. Seeing how someone's career or reputation can be broken simply due to one small error (which might be from way back when) is a powerful way to illustrate how far-reaching the effects of social media can be. It might not be representative of who they are as an adult – but it will still be out there for anyone to see and they could still form an opinion of them based on a comment made in the ignorance of youth.

4 **Talk about consequences.** Comments made on social media when they're, say, 16 or 17, might have repercussions a lot later on when it can have a greater impact on their life and livelihood, but so too can posts that contain images. I've made sure my girls understand that a flippant comment or iffy photo posted now by themselves or by other people could make things difficult for them in future. Posting a picture with your boobs out might seem funny now – and yes, they're your boobs and very nice boobs and all of that – but if you want to become a lawyer in a few years' time it won't necessarily do you any favours or promote the image your employer is looking for.

Continued overleaf →

TOO MUCH INFORMATION...

What our kids are being exposed to that they don't understand came home to me recently when Ava came to me and asked whether I'd seen something with some hashtags that neither of us recognized. She'd googled them because everyone was using them and wanted to know what it was all about. They were to do with eating disorders, and I was horrified.

As a parent with some control, I can block specific sites and hashtags that I know about and that I think are inappropriate for my kids, but I wouldn't have blocked those specific hashtags because I knew nothing about them. And that's the thing: it's not black and white and there are so many shades of grey. People she knows are looking at this stuff and sending it through to her, and I'm not going to block her friends, and I'm not going to ask her to do that either.

And it can also happen with innocent googling for a legitimate purpose; while Hero was doing home school and looking stuff up online something came up about a child with cancer and the mum was asking for money to save their life. Hero was distraught - and yet that didn't come up in any of my parental blocks either. So the only way I can counteract any of this is by keeping the lines of communication open and talking about all these things that they are seeing and helping them to understand what's real, what's not, what to believe, and what to avoid if it is exploiting them in some way. It means we are having some pretty big conversations at the moment, but they've got to know they can come to me and get an answer.

Also, it's not as simple as hitting delete if you change your mind about something you've posted - by the time you go to remove it, it might have been shared and screenshotted, and then it's out of your control. This is relevant to us all - no matter how old we are. And with cameraphones snapping everywhere, it's a conversation that is worth having with other people about sharing images of you, too.

5   **Ask yourself what you are being sold and why**. This is another one that's useful for all of us. The thing about social media is that much of the time we are simply seeing what people want us to see. Is what someone has posted the full (or even real) story, or is it simply a snapshot of a situation that's not representative of the whole? Maybe people have posted to make themselves look good. Or to make other people look bad. Or maybe to make a point. Or to make themselves feel better about something by giving the impression that everything is amazing when it's not. It can be all too easy to think everyone is having a better time than you are when you scroll through social media, so learning to distinguish between what you see and what is reality is so important.

6   **Don't rely on parental controls**. Another thing I have learned when it comes to kids on devices is that it's also really important to be aware of the limitations that are in place on these. In fact, I am realizing more and more that I am the parental control because there are so many ways into things you might not even have thought of, and that aren't covered by the social media servers and moderation. Again, this goes back to the point about communication – if you can talk to you child without judgement, you will have a better idea of what they are looking at online.

It's difficult: we want to protect our kids and keep them away from all this, yet there are so many positive reasons for them to be online too. It's like the tail wagging the dog. So the best thing we can do is empower them to make sensible choices. Remember, children use social media differently from adults. Don't expect them to hide their pics in the same places you would, or talk in the same language, or on the same forums you do. You might not be able to match them on tech, but you can most definitely familiarize yourself and keep up with them. I have heard mums say, 'My child would never post that kind of thing', when I know for a fact they are wrong. They're just looking in the wrong place. It's not about catching your child out; it's about keeping them safe. Put it this way, if there were photos still out there of you when you were 16 or 17, wouldn't you be mortified?

We can't stick our heads in the sand and just let them get on with. We should always make it our business to know what they are seeing and posting. So just as we worry about whether they are eating, sleeping, happy, doing homework, what they are being exposed to online and how they process that information is another thing to add to that list.

LIMIT TIME ONLINE

Online schooling changed my approach to time online. I went from really trying to monitor and pull things back to encouraging my children to get online and get their schoolwork done. It's not always reasonable to set a limit as I have done in the past, as if they haven't finished their homework on time, then you're actually creating a bigger problem. Limiting gaming time or time spent on socials, all of that is helpful, as is (if it works for you and your child) linking or syncing your phones so you can see which sites they're looking at, or know how long they've been on a particular app. Ultimately, you can ban everything outright and push it all underground, or you can talk about what's going on and set limits around use. In our house, the rules are: no phones at the table, at family time, or in rooms overnight. It's not a bad rule for the grown-ups either!

Talk about body image

I find body image a fascinating subject. Growing up in the Filipino community, we had different ideals of beauty, so it's really interesting to hear what my conventionally white friends might find attractive compared to my friends who have more exotic looks. There's definitely no one size fits all; some people are desperate to get a tan whereas others want to have lighter skin; some people perm their hair curly, but others perm their hair straight ... the list goes on.

Having that chat with your kids about body image is really important, however they identify, and I think it is just as important to remember as adults too. These are the things I have said to my girls on this subject.

1   **Never compare yourself to others**. We are all made differently. Embrace your uniqueness and make the best of yourself. Sometimes you might feel rubbish, but hauling yourself out of bed and into the shower can often make the difference. Putting on your favourite outfit, your make-up. Getting out for a walk. Body and mind are so powerfully linked. You have to know how to make yourself happy. Comparing yourself to others saps joy from everything.

2   **Be realistic**. Wishful thinking is never going to mean that your legs are suddenly going to be eight inches longer overnight. So, decide what you think is desirable, figure out what is achievable while staying happy and healthy, then find the happy medium between the two. It's actually the things that I would have wanted to change growing up that are some of the reasons why I've become successful as an adult. I remember at 19 trying to get into the West-End show *Miss Saigon*, but I had been turned down twice before. I did a lot of soul-searching and was insecure about whether I had the talent to do it. When I was finally accepted, the choreographer told me I had been too tall for the previous casts, but fitted this one perfectly (my dance partner was 6'6"). I then went on to be part of the anniversary year which saw the original ensemble return, so I got to perform with the people who had inspired me to be there in the first place. Sometimes your face/body doesn't fit and it can be a good thing!

3   **Accept your body for what it is and celebrate it**. I'm never going to be ten feet tall, and buying clothes for people who are ten feet tall is always going to end in tears and disaster. At the same time, I have friends who say they wish they could wear the clothes I do because I'm curvy, but they know they just won't work for them. Whatever your body shape you can enhance it by going to a gym or finding another form of exercise you enjoy. I made sure that I signed my girls up to gymnastics because I want their bodies to be strong. Not thin bodies, but empowered, strong, capable bodies.

4   **We come in different shapes and sizes**. It can take a lot of self-love and confidence to understand that no one body type is the optimum. In the interim you really have to watch your children, explain things to them, and celebrate different body types. Show them that you could have six women who all weigh exactly the same, whether it's eight stone or ten stone, and their shapes will all be completely different.

5   **No appetite for diets**. I don't want the word 'diet' used in my house. In fact, I took this to such an extreme that at one point I wouldn't even say Diet Coke – it's still known as 'DC' even now. I don't know so much from a boy's point of view, but for girls I think women constantly sucking their tummies in or complaining they look fat can be so damaging. The only reason I bought scales for my house was to weigh baggage. It's really important that children realize those numbers do not equate to happiness.

6   **Times change**. There's a fascinating historical lesson in talking to your children about beauty ideals over the years. In days gone by, people wanted to be pale and rounded: it showed they were well-fed and didn't have to work in the fields. Now obviously it's switched around, and if you have a tan it shows you can afford to go on holiday and so on. Fashions change. It's cultural, it's evolutionary.

7   **Get real**. When I was growing up I never looked at a copy of my mum's *Woman's Own* and thought, I must get thighs like that. But now girls are exposed to so much. They see bodies of trophy wives and pole dancers. They see doctored images that are passed off as reality – and then they wonder why they can never match up. It's a great idea to show a child a doctored image along with the original that hasn't been retouched. (The first thing Hero would ask is why has she done that? Why has she straightened her nose? Changed her hair? That's what she would pick up on more so than the reason behind it.)

8   **Do things for YOU and not other people**. I want my girls to understand why they might want to do something – is it their choice? Are they're feeling pressured into it because their friends say they should do it? Or do they think it will make them more attractive to a particular person or get them a job if they go along with it?

Continued overleaf →

It's important to me that my girls understand what bodies can achieve rather than just how they look. I asked Ava: Who's more attractive, the girl who got a bit muddy and is running around on the playing field, or the one who is preening and won't come out of the dressing room? Ava's in cheer squad – she's the base, strong legs, she has to catch everybody, and I remind her that her strength holds everyone else up. Her body creates the foundation. She's vital. If she doesn't catch them, the whole thing falls apart.

9   **You are not alone**. It's also worth remembering that many things that people find hard to cope with, such as bad skin, are things that everyone goes through. I've got stretch marks – my badge of honour. I've shown them to Ava and said to her, Look, you will get stretch marks because I have stretch marks, and it is hereditary. Let me show you what they look like, let me explain why you get them – let's look at the science behind them rather than just saying, Oh my god they're so ugly, I hate them.

It's not always easy to embrace things that wobble or don't look picture-perfect. So show your children the things that you think society wouldn't necessarily celebrate and show them you're okay with them. It comes back to making the best of what you've got and thinking what would I like to be able to do with this body? And it doesn't have to be all about bleaching it, and straightening it, and waxing it because you feel the pressure of doing that. When Ava says she wants to be a capable woman who can do lots of different things, I'll say, Okay then maybe you should just try lots of different things. It's good to learn tenacity and patience and work at something, and I try to guide her in that direction, away from a preoccupation about body image.

And in the end it's horses for courses. I say to my girls, you can be the best peach, the most amazing peach, the juiciest peach in the fruit bowl and somebody might come along and still want a pear.

'No one is going to be everybody's cup of tea and they're not going to be yours. But you can always be the best version of yourself.'

Be a keeper of feelings and fears

Boundaries are so important. They make everyone feel safe. Whether you have a blended family like mine, a nuclear family, or any other kind of family unit, boundaries are vital for anyone with children.

There are days when we all feel overwhelmed. It's hard to know where to begin tackling the overload our minds are experiencing or the emotions we're feeling. When growing up, a pet hate of mine was how confusing it could be when adults would try and hide things from me when I knew something was wrong, and then, they would dismiss it, or say how easy I had it being a child: 'Wait till you're older and have to pay bills'; 'Wait till you have real worries'. Looking back, my parents got it right. They never overshared their worries and I never felt I had to parent them or that they relied on me in any way.

However, I've seen many times that this isn't the case for a lot of people and, as a result, it is something I try really hard to remember as an adult and a mum – that your feelings as a child are the only ones you have, you have no basis for comparison. And what feels like a pressure, a problem, or a challenge can be extremely overwhelming. It's all relative.

Having an adult dismiss your issue as insignificant can cause a small person to feel unworthy, or not recognized. Equally, many parents and adults offload or use their children in the role of friend, advisor, agony aunt. Not having emotional boundaries results in a child who people-pleases as an adult, and feels responsible for everyone else's happiness with no sense of self.

I show my girls two glasses all the time: one is a pint glass (representing me); one is a child-sized cup (them). I fill the children's glass with water. The water represents their worries, fears, pressures. I then get them to pour the water from the kid's cup into the pint glass (me).

Continued overleaf →

I make a point of showing them how much more water the pint glass can hold. I, as their mum, am there to carry them, hold their worries, and still have loads of room left on top for everything and everyone else. I then fill my pint glass to the brim, the one that represents me and my worries or fears, and then try to pour the water back into their empty child's cup. Naturally the water overflows and spills everywhere.

It's a beautiful visual cue and representation for children to see how it's the job of the parents to carry them, and not the other way round. And although it's okay to say you're sad, you had a bad day, you have a lot going on, and to normalize those feelings, it is equally important for adults not to overburden their children with adult issues and worries. It's important to acknowledge that no one can be happy all of the time, and equally important to show and establish a firm boundary for your child to make them feel safe.

Relationship woes, financial struggles, upset, inappropriate information ... a child cannot help you. They are the helpless ones in these scenarios and burdening them is setting them up to face further issues down the line. The above example is also good for adults to use for themselves, although they in turn might need to find a bigger glass to pour into – that is, a friend, a therapist, or a partner.

HOW TO

Talk about basic finance

Many kids find the concept of large amounts of money impossible to process. It's not really surprising when you think that the sums needed to buy a car, or a flat, or a house are way (way!) out of the realms of anything they will have encountered. So I'm a big believer in starting small when it comes to helping them to understand money in real terms – it's easier for them to keep it real.

The way I've taught my girls is when we have been shopping for the food bank. I'll say, Here's £5, go into the shop and put a meal together. When they came out the first time they were both elated with what they had managed to put together, and shocked at what that amount of money could – or couldn't – buy. Next time they started heading to the own-brands, realizing the premium that you pay for branded goods that isn't always viable on a tight budget.

1   **Credit versus debit**. I've taught my kids the difference between credit cards and debit cards. Why there's great pleasure in cutting up credit cards, why everyone's going to try and offer one to you, why it's going to be such an attractive prospect, and why it can end up costing you twice as much in the long run.

2   **Balancing act**. Another thing I talk about with my girls is the difference between being in the black and being in the red – basic finance, but again in a way they can understand. And they've definitely taken it on board. Hero is so funny, she keeps saying I don't ever want to be in the red, I never want to be in the red. Am I going to be in the red if I do this?

3   **Pocket money**. I don't give this to my kids, they have to earn it. Ava has seven piano pupils now, so she's got her own money coming in, and when she goes and buys one of those profoundly expensive bubble teas, on her head be it. It's up to her. It's no different from me buying a designer coffee from Starbucks. If she wants to go and get her bubble tea with the money she's earned, she'll feel it and know exactly how much of her time it's worth. I had seven pupils from the age of 13 and it taught me so much – it taught me how to budget my money and it also meant that when I had saved up and bought an item I looked after it, I enjoyed it more. I think this is really important. Some people say children shouldn't be bothered with things that don't concern them, but it becomes serious when the stakes are high, and if you're a child the stakes are lower and it is just all fun, the best way to learn. Ava isn't paying rent on the piano for the lessons, she doesn't have to worry about the heating for her pupils or the music. She just has to give her time and she enjoys it.

4   **Younger kids**. If they are old enough to write then they are old enough to learn! To get little ones started you can get them to write down their pocket money or what's in their piggy bank and then what they spend it on. The concept of money can be confusingly abstract and this is the perfect way to start teaching them about incomings and outgoings.

'I'm a big believer in starting small when it comes to helping them to understand money in real terms.'

HOW TO
Talk about drink-spiking

It's really easy to think that if you are careful this is something you can avoid. But trust me, it's not, and this can happen to grown-up, streetwise women just as easily as it can to young, less wordly wise girls. Forewarned is forearmed, so I used a simple trick to show my girls just how easily it can happen.

1   Don't tell them you are planning it (obviously), but sit down and have a chat. It can be about anything you like.

2   Make sure you each have a drink in front of you.

3   As you engage them in conversation, surreptitiously drop a peppercorn into their drink.

4   Change the chat to talking about the dangers of drinks being spiked.

5   When they protest that they know, point out the peppercorn/s in their glass.

It's simple and effective. Ava loved it; she was shocked! 'I did not see you do that. And boom, you've done it three or four times'. That's how easy it is. Lesson learned.

I know exactly how scary it can be because it happened to me back in the days when I was in the band. We were in a club, I recall a friend holding out his hand asking if I was going to be sick, and that was pretty much my last memory. Thankfully I was with friends who looked after me. One of the girls took me back and put me to bed. I remember her leaving and seeing that the door was open, but I couldn't even get out of bed to close it. It took a full 24 hours to recover.

Rather than put fear into my girls about this, I've tried to empower them with ways to protect themselves and still have a nice time. I've taught Ava the rule of thumb is you don't ever go back to a drink that you've left unattended or out of your sight for any amount of time. I've said I don't care if it's a really expensive cocktail, I will reimburse her, but you don't walk away from a drink and you don't take drinks from someone you don't know who brings it over. You have to give yourself the best chance. Take your drink to the loo with you when you go; girls will understand what you're doing because there will be a dozen others in that loo holding a drink, but you don't ever touch a drink that's been left on the table.

Talk about questioning authority

It goes without saying there is a time and a place when it's appropriate to question someone who has greater authority than you – as an adult and as a child. If you're challenging something because you don't fancy doing it, you're being obstinate or contrary, then most likely this stance is going to land you in trouble. But there are absolutely times when it is the right thing to do.

It might be because it's something you strongly believe in – a prime example is Greta Thunberg – and because you feel something needs to change. A friend's daughter was unhappy with her school's recycling policy. By coming up with solutions to the issues that she saw in it, and presenting them in a constructive and non-combative manner, she got them to revise it. Or it might be because something is making you feel uncomfortable. We are taught to listen to our teachers and respect our elders. As a result of this I got into trouble, and certainly found myself in positions where I couldn't speak to my parents. I don't want that for my girls. There will always be exceptions to rules and there will always be times when you should listen to your gut and make a stand. And I want my girls to know they can.

These are my golden rules for when it's okay to challenge authority:

1   Some things challenge us and push us out of our comfort zones in a good and constructive way. But if something you've been told to do makes you uncomfortable, then it's probably wrong.

2   Whether it's a teacher, or a police officer, or an elder, you should still be able to question them. Why are they asking you to do this? I have said to my girls that even if someone wants you to do something that you feel just isn't right, don't do it – it's fine.

3   A forthright 'NO!' can work well. 'No' is a small word, but is often very hard to say. More so for women, as it's ingrained in us that saying no makes us bossy, disagreeable, difficult, so practise saying it. It's a powerful word. It means you are forthright, know your own mind, won't be forced or coerced. If you are being forced into something, feel uncomfortable, or just don't agree, then 'No!'

4   If you don't feel you can say no, make an excuse or say, 'I need to speak to my mum first'.

HOW TO

Talk about what's happening in the world

It's always been really important to me to explain what's happening in the news as best as I can to my girls. There are many people who think you should turn it off the second that children walk in the room – especially if it's sad or bad news – but I don't understand that. You're attaching your emotion to whatever is being reported, but actually, *not* knowing the full story can be far scarier.

How you talk about the news with your children is always the crucial thing. As a child, whenever it was time for me to go to bed, I'd take an interest in the news, mainly so I could stay downstairs a bit longer! 'It's really important!' I'd insist. But what I saw could also be very confusing, because we didn't ever discuss it.

I always wondered why, during the Troubles in Ireland, whenever the newsreaders were talking about the IRA or Gerry Adams, they'd show a darkened room with a plant on top of a filing cabinet and use a weird, automated-sounding voice. My parents didn't explain why this was (it was because the BBC had banned interviews with representatives of Sinn Fein and several other pro-Republican groups) and somehow that made it even scarier at a time when you would walk down Oxford Street and there were no bins because the IRA were putting bombs in them.

There are plenty of things happening today that are also discomfiting enough without picking up half-truths and creating worst-case scenarios in your imagination that are far worse than the reality. So it's important to me to talk to my girls about what's going on and what it all really means.

My tips on educating your kids about current affairs:

1   **Allow your children access to the news but control how they get it.** These days news is everywhere – on newspaper headlines, the radio, the TV, online – so it's even more important to give children context and explanations when they might only get a tiny slither of the story. You can let them sit in front of a channel that's delivering news almost as entertainment, or you can be that channel and explain the situation in words that you think are appropriate for your child.

2   **Talk about difficult stories and make sure they understand the context.** Lots of events are hard enough for adults to process, let alone children, but it's good to find a way to talk about things so they are able to share their worries and fears rather than keeping it all bottled up. You might explain that something very sad has happened and a lot of people are feeling very upset about it, and we can feel sad about it too. But you have to contextualize it, empower them by offering possible solutions where they are valid.

3   **Try not to let your own emotion colour how you explain things**. Obviously it's fine and appropriate to be upset if something is sad or scary, but catastrophizing won't help anyone.

4   **Make sure they know that they can always discuss things with you.**

5   **Give them access to child-friendly news sources so that they can learn about things independently, too.** There are also brilliant publications designed for kids like *First News* and *The Week Junior,* which deliver current affairs in bite-sized chunks, which means they can read up themselves and feel really empowered by being able to tell you about the things they have read about.

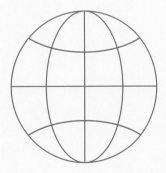

Talk about pronouns

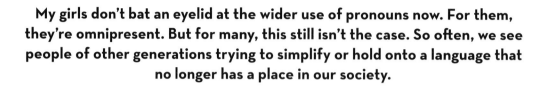

My girls don't bat an eyelid at the wider use of pronouns now. For them, they're omnipresent. But for many, this still isn't the case. So often, we see people of other generations trying to simplify or hold onto a language that no longer has a place in our society.

When I watch old movies with my girls thinking they'll love them as much as I did, it's fascinating to see how a lack of nostalgia and context of the era very quickly exposes how wrong we got it; for instance, *Pretty Woman*, *9 to 5*, practically every James Bond film and, before that, films from our parents' generation, *Casablanca*, *Gone with the Wind*, and many more. They do belong to a different time and although you can't erase the problems, you can learn from them. Many think of this as white-washing the past; others blame an overly woke generation. Think of it this way: the bottom-slapping and wolf whistles, the 'empowering way' Julia Roberts' character walks into a shop to spend the money her client has given her ... were these things ever *empowering*?

She/he/they	He/her/them	Possessive (her/his/their/s)	Herself/himself/themself
Ae	Aer	Aer/s	Aerself
Co	Co	Cos	Coself
E/Ey	Em	Eir/s	Eirself
En	En	Ens	Enself
Fae	Faer	Faer/s	Faerself
Per	Per	Pers	Perself
Ve	Ver	Vis	Viself
Xie (or Zie)	Hir	Hirs	Hirself
Yo	Yo	Yos	Yoself
Ze	Zir	Zir	Zirself

Times have changed. We have more information, more diversity, and more visibility. Today, we can be whoever we want to be. Use the pronouns that people wish you to use and foster respect and inclusivity. No one should assume another person's gender, pronoun, or sexuality.

Add your own to your bio on emails or social media for ease all round. If you're not sure of a person's pronouns, ask! If you get it wrong, apologize, correct yourself, and move on.

And while we're fostering inclusivity, let's take a closer look at LGBTQIA+

L is for **lesbian**: A woman who is primarily attracted to other women.

G is for **gay**: A man who is primarily attracted to other men.

B is for **bisexual**: Someone who is attracted to both their own and the opposite gender.

T is for **transgender**: Someone whose gender identity is different from the sex they were assigned at birth. Historically T has also been used for 'transsexual', someone who has changed gender through hormones/surgery. BUT this is an outdated term and should no longer be used.

Q is for **queer**: A useful term that encapsulates those who are part of the LGBTQ+ community and inclusive of many different identities within it.

Q is for **questioning**: For those who are discovering or exploring their gender identity or their sexual orientation.

I is for **intersex**: Someone whose sexual make-up (chromosomes) or anatomy doesn't fall within the traditional 'male' or 'female' markers.

A is for **ally**: Can be someone within the community who supports an individual with a different identity to them, or someone outside the LGBTQ+ community who supports or advocates for those within.

A is for **asexual**: Someone who does not feel sexual attraction or desire at all. This should not be confused with celibacy which is an active choice to refrain from sexual activity.

P is for **pansexual**: Someone who feels attraction (be it sexual, physical, or romantic) to people of all gender identities rather than just those who fit the standard gender binary.

G is for **genderfluid**: A person who can identify at any time as different genders.

N is for **nonbinary** (gender queer): Someone who identifies as a gender that is not exclusively male or female; namely, outside the binaries.

4

Being a Grown-up

Ava, aged 9, and Hero, aged 6, opening an account with their earnings. Teach kids about finance from a young age

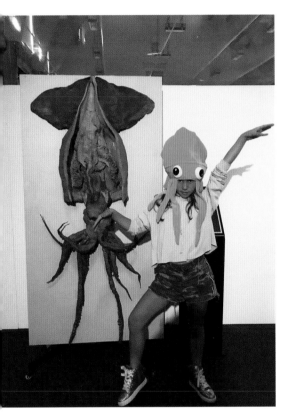

Hero, aged 6. Science nerd.
Understanding how the
world works encourages
confidence

Ava, aged 9. Information
is key. Follow your passion.
Mini marine biologist

HOW TO
Take criticism

Whether it's at school, at work, or even just among friends or family, there will be times when we get feedback that we don't necessarily like, and learning how to handle criticism is definitely a major life skill.

Constructive criticism (which is given to help us do better at whatever it is next time round) can be really useful, but it doesn't always mean it's easy to take.

Unconstructive criticism ... is harder still.

Our reactions can often depend on what's being said (and by whom). We might feel:

- **Grateful**; if this feedback has something useful to take away from it, and we can see it's going to make us better/do better in the long run.

- **Angry**; if we don't think it's justified.

- **Upset**; because if you've worked hard on something it can be hard to hear that there's more still to do – even if the suggestions are ultimately helpful.

- **Defensive**; this is a natural reaction if you think the criticism is unfair. But it's always good to take a pause, a step back, or a deep breath before acting on your emotions – to take a cooling-off period, if you like – to stop yourself lashing out and saying something you might regret.

THINGS TO REMEMBER

- It's honest feedback – that's a good thing. It gives you the chance to make positive changes.

- Try not to take it as a personal attack. Most of the time it won't be.

- Learn from it – not only how to do things differently but how things that you do or say are perceived by other people.

- But if it is not constructive, and the criticism is unwarranted or unjustified, be the bigger person and walk away without losing it or stooping to their level. You can calmly thank them for any nuggets that might be useful or constructive but try not to react to the rest; it won't get you anywhere and showing them you're not rattled (even if you are!) will only reflect positively on you.

To me the great secret of taking criticism is to pause, take a step back from the moment, reflect on what's been said, and ask yourself if you have really done a good job or is what you are hearing justified?

If someone says to me 'That was incredible' and I know in my heart of hearts that it wasn't, it makes me mistrustful of either their level of expertise or them generally, because I think they're just trying to be nice to me – and if they're doing that they're not really going to help me learn from my mistakes.

If criticism is justified, and I can acknowledge that, I can take it because I know it myself already. Then you just need to ask the question, How can I be better?

> *I have shown my girls criticism of me and talked about when it's constructive or when it's best to just hold my head high and walk away. You can read a hundred great comments and it will be the one bad one that you remember. I still remember someone online saying I had 'No class, fat arse'. But I've taught my kids that if it's an insult, it's not a critique.*
>
> *When the girls and I do live TikToks, we often ask questions in them, so have to read the comments. One person once commented, 'Hi, disappointments'. If I had responded to say 'We're doing this free music class to help educate the nation and that's the best you've got?' it wouldn't have changed anything. I explained this to the girls, and so instead we use humour to deflect these types of comments. Now in the morning we often come downstairs and announce, 'Hi, disappointments'. We've made a joke of it and we can all move on.*

HANDLING REJECTION

If you've worked really hard at something and it comes back as a no, it's really tough. I've felt that disappointment and frustration myself. Sometimes it's just that whatever you've done (be it a piece of work, a performance, or an interview) isn't good enough. If so, you have to ask yourself whether that's because you didn't do your best on this occasion so next time you need to try harder. Be honest with yourself about what you might have been able to do differently. If you learn from it then you're effectively turning it into a positive.

But sometimes you will have given it everything you can and you know you simply couldn't have done any better. If that's the case it may be simply that this subject/job or whatever just isn't for you. And there's never any harm in realizing areas that are not your strength. (We all have them!)

HOW TO
Take a compliment

We all like to feel accepted and valued by our peers, but sometimes taking that compliment that we've been hoping for is one of the hardest things to do!

Think back to the last time someone complimented you – what did you do? It's the most natural thing in the world to be embarrassed and respond to a compliment with a question: You look lovely/Do I really? Or by brushing it off: Lovely dress/What this old thing?

But if someone has taken the time and effort to say something lovely to you, it's always going to be better (and more polite) if you can accept their compliment gracefully. And rather than doing yourself down, allow yourself to feel good in the process!

In the past I often found myself being quite apologetic, but then I worked in America for a year and if you do that there, they take you at your word. So people might say, 'I saw you perform and it was really good' and I'd reply, 'Oh no, I just threw it together' and they'd just look at me and say 'Oh'. It made me realize that mine wasn't the right reaction at all and I was just talking myself down. We almost half-expect it here, as it's a very British trait, but in America it just didn't translate. If I said, 'No, no, I'm not very good at that' they would reply 'Okay, then it's better if you don't do it again.' It was real culture shock, which is why I learned to say thank you!

There is a simple way to do this that you can learn too: **Practise saying thank you!**

Thank you. Full stop.

Two small words that it seems can be surprisingly hard to say. But practice makes perfect and if you're not comfortable doing this out loud, you can do it in your head until you get used to it. But make a commitment to yourself to respond with a thank you before anything else.

HOW TO

Be graceful in defeat (or a good loser)

We can all deal with stuff when we're having a fine old time, but when we're not we can stumble, fall apart, or we can rise to it, step up, and deal with it. And trust me, there are plenty of times when I want to fall apart but I can't, because if I wallow in my misery who's going to mop up my kids and pick them up emotionally?

Being gracious in defeat is a skill in its own right, because who wants to lose? We are not programmed that way. And it's hard! I've worked with Olympians now and seen how it sits with them and it's understandable; if you've trained to win, why would you be happy if you don't?

But it happens to us all at some point. It might not be a competition. It could be a job, or a relationship, or a friendship. Whatever the situation, it's important to learn to deal with it. So, put your pride to one side, as these are skills that are invaluable at any age.

- It's okay to be sad and to show your kids that you're sad.

- Explain why you feel that way: it didn't go the way you wanted it to go and you are upset or disappointed.

- Set yourself a time limit – whether it's ten minutes, an hour or a day or two (depending on what's happened) – then decide what you are going to do to move forward after that.

The last bit is really important, because if you're going to be that person who, four weeks later, is still sitting on the sofa crying into the ice cream because something didn't go your way, you need to find a way to pick yourself up and the strength to move on.

Deal with FOMO

No matter how old we are, there will always be times when we feel like we are being left out of things, or that everyone is having a better time than we are. But there's no doubt that FOMO – the Fear of Missing Out – has hit new heights since the advent of social media.

When I was a teenager you might have heard that there was a party at the weekend, but your FOMO could only stretch as far as your wildest imagination, or what someone had (usually) exaggerated the best part of the evening to be. Now we are presented with images live from the event or in the immediate aftermath that imply everyone is having the time of their lives. But often – oh, so often – that really is not the case.

It's not just kids who feel they are missing out, though. Lockdown during Covid-19 might have made things easier for a while because no one was out having fun, but before and after that there have definitely been times when I've felt the FOMO creeping in. I'll see pictures of a group of my mates and think I could have been invited, they didn't invite me ... Later on, though, I'll find out they just bumped into each other or it just wasn't as Machiavellian a gathering as I had decided it must be in my head. It's all too easy to react and let your thoughts run wild.

'Remember that what you see won't be the whole story — or even the real story.'

WHAT YOU SHOULD REMEMBER

Every picture tells a story … but remember that what you see won't be the whole story – or even the real story. If it's on social media it's likely that you'll only see what's supposedly the best part or the edited 'highlights' – perhaps who's going out, but not necessarily where they're going. Even those hints can bring on pure FOMO, but as with so many things in life, the grass isn't necessarily greener.

It's not always easy: Ava, whose motto is 'You can't believe that because it's on Instagram', still inevitably gets FOMO.

WHAT CAN I DO ABOUT IT?

It's important to remember that happiness doesn't have to mean being out or surrounded by other people; if you can find happiness at home doing something you enjoy (a good book, a great movie …) or hanging out with a friend, then whatever you're potentially being sold is irrelevant. Everything is easier to deal with if we are in a good place ourselves.

So the simple answer to this question is to find things that make us happy; the reason we get FOMO is because we believe whoever we are watching is in a better place than we are. But are they really? That's the $64,000 question – and the answer is generally 'no'.

Ultimately the lesson is: be happy in your own environment and with your own choices. Finding that confidence might take time, but it will make a world of difference when you get there. In fact, often these days I realize I have POMO, or the Pleasure of Missing Out. Would I rather be at the party or at home watching *The Crown* with a bucket of popcorn? No contest.

HOW TO
Handle screen time

There's no doubt that working out how much screen time your children should have is a thankless task, but if we're honest with ourselves, the amount of time we spend on screens as adults is just as big an issue.

So when it comes to laying down the ground rules, you're not only in danger of driving yourself mad, but also of ending up a walking contradiction; my very young son picked up the charger and attached it to my phone. He knew what to do because he'd watched me do it a hundred times.

If they're seeing you with your head in your phone, don't then tell them off for having their heads in their phones. As much as it's do as I say not as I do, ultimately they'll take their cues 90 per cent from watching you, and 10 per cent from what you say, so you have to set the first example. Meaningful – and limited – screen time is the way forward, whatever your age.

THE LITTLE BIG SCREEN

We are not a big TV household but we do get together for event viewing and really use the time to focus on one thing. We'll watch a movie or a box set or something like Blue Planet together and make a big thing of it. I let them watch a concert while I was working - gave them popcorn, said Hero could stay up an hour later, made it feel like an event, so it was more special than just any old telly or free childcare.

So, here are a few thoughts on how to live harmoniously with tech and your children:

- Be on your phone from dawn to dusk. If you never put it down then you are showing your kids that that's acceptable. And it's not good for you either, particularly when you are trying to switch off at the end of the day.

- Have screens on just as background. If you want to watch something on TV, watch the programme, then switch it off afterwards. If you want to send an email or look something up, do so, but don't automatically browse through all your apps afterwards.

- Make screen time purposeful (for you as well as for them). Make it a destination point rather than something that's just always there floating around, because then you just can never switch off from it.

- Set a time limit and stick to it. If you find it tricky there are plenty of screen time programmes/internet blockers that will help.

I massively limit time for the kids on laptops and iPads too. It's so easy to spend time browsing absent-mindedly – and I know this because it is definitely something that I do too. I say to the girls it's a book you can never put down, it's not a book with an ending, so it just goes on and on infinitely. But I also use social media a great deal for my work and so a lot of the time I need to be online, and this is hard to explain to my girls when they want to know why is yours work and mine isn't?

I do want my children to be involved in the world around them and to keep up with what's happening, and I know the news doesn't wait on the hour every hour, it's constant. But I was still really quite shocked to see how much time they would spend on their screens if I didn't put a limit on it, so it's about finding a balance. We make sure that there's always a reason for them to be online – finding something out, or a limited amount of social media every day. And we talk about it, too. I also try to keep them busy with other things even if they think I'm nagging – I *am* nagging, I'm their mum and that's my job!

Write a letter

In the age of emails, texts, and WhatsApp messages, letters seem to be becoming increasingly rare. But I'm a big fan. Getting a letter is such a nice thing, so I have always made sure that both my children and I write thank yous the old-fashioned way. They are important because they acknowledge that someone took the time to pick something out that they thought you would like, so the least you can do in return is take the time to thank them properly.

Gifts are something I feel very strongly about. It's absolutely not about how much you spend or what you buy. It's all about the thought that's gone into it.

1   Make sure you spell the name/s of the recipient correctly.

2   Thank them for what they bought.

3   Always add a line about why you particularly like it or when you plan to use it – the detail is really important in making it personal and showing you have thought about it. The last thing you want the recipient to think is that you are just dashing off a load of identical letters with <insert name here> in them as fast as you can. They put thought into buying you something. You put thought into thanking them.

4   Sign off properly.

Hero got a typewriter for her birthday and she's been typing her thank yous, which is very sweet to see, but also frustrating for us both as, in her words, 'You can't delete anything!'

SYMPATHY LETTERS

These can be really difficult to write, but they are also really important. They acknowledge that someone is going through loss and a hugely difficult time, and they show support. In terms of general layout and showing that you are thinking of them, the principle of writing the letter is much the same. As well as expressing your sadness for their loss, add personal detail too. I wrote to a friend who had lost her father recently and, as well as saying that I was sorry and was thinking about her, I added a line about her dad that I knew would make her smile. I wanted to share happy memories as well as offer support.

Write a CV

I've already started talking to my kids about CVs and interviews. It might not sound relevant to a child, but you are never too young to think about what you're good at and how to sell yourself.

Knowing how to put together a CV is great for communication skills and also really useful practice for university applications or for putting yourself forward for opportunities at school or weekend/summer jobs. In a CV you want to be able to give a snapshot of who you are and what you've achieved (without writing a 20-page essay), so you really have to think about what you are trying to say about yourself, what you have to offer, and how best to show this in just a few paragraphs.

So, here's a quick-fire guide to what you need to know when writing a CV:

• It should never be longer than two A4 pages.

• Check the spelling and punctuation – then check it again!

• Add any qualifications you have – music exams, dance, sport – even if they're not directly relevant to what you are applying for, as they do show the effort and work that you have put in to reach a high standard.

• Don't add anything that's not true – you will always get caught out.

• Don't just list what you've done, add the skills that you've learned from your achievements, such as good organization, communication, how to work as part of a team.

• It's not just about results and experience; extracurricular activities are worth including, too. It's good to be able to demonstrate that you have hobbies because people like to know what your interests are and you might need to be able to talk about them in an interview. Someone I know always used to add punting to his, and it's stuck with me because unless you are going for a job in Venice or Cambridge it's not likely to be any use at all, but he said it was a real talking point and before he knew it, he'd created an opportunity to engage in a conversation.

Apply for a job

This is another major life skill and one that so many people never get taught properly, which means they either end up repeating their mistakes over and over, or learning (eventually) through bitter experience.

This is something that's relevant for everyone – adults looking to change career, or even children who aren't yet not old enough for the job market. Knowing how to put together a decent application and get through an interview are massively useful at all stages in life. It's a skill that's applicable whether you're at school and applying to be a prefect (that cover letter is CRUCIAL), or putting together university entry forms and personal statements, as well as looking for employment at any level.

These are the important things to remember (always!):

- Read through the advert or job description carefully. After years of being made to do comprehension at school and not getting the point of it at all, I now realize THIS is what it was for! It's all about extracting the relevant information from the text and formulating your answers from there.

- Make bullet points of every desirable skill, attribute, or experience that is being asked for – the ones that are must-haves and also the ones that are optional.

- For each bullet point think of one or two things you have done, or skills that you have, that demonstrate your ability in this area.

- Don't worry if you are applying for something you haven't done before. Think about transferable skills – relevant skills and experience that you already have that could be used in this role. What have you done successfully elsewhere and in a different role that shows that you can do what they are looking for? For example, if you want to be a prefect, think about times when you might have shown good leadership in other areas, such as captaining a sports team.

When you write up your application you MUST:

- Double-check your spelling and punctuation. I cannot stress enough how important this is. Sloppy mistakes will never impress a potential employer.

- Always find out the name of the person to whom you are sending your letter/CV and make sure you spell it correctly. Mentioning absolutely no names, I used to work with someone who would throw anything where their name was misspelled straight into the bin. 'If they don't care enough to get it right then I don't care enough to read it.' Harsh but true.

- Make sure you get the name of the organization you are applying to right, too (there is no point talking about how much you want to work for, say, Cancer Research, if you are applying for a job on a magazine. This happens A LOT when people simply cut and paste from letters they have used for previous applications. Beware of this and always make sure you tailor any application to the specific thing you are applying for at that point.

- Try to add a line or two about the organization you're applying to and why you would like to be a part of it. This shows genuine interest and that you've really taken time to think about the role.

'These principles work throughout life, whether you are applying to be part of something at school or for the job of your dreams.'

NEXT STEPS

If you've got all that right, the next step is generally an interview. This bit can be daunting, especially if you don't have experience of being asked questions by a group of teachers/lecturers/would-be employers. As ever, my motto is practise, practise, practise. Being prepared is half the battle.

I've already started to role-play interviews with my girls, or at least to throw in on-the-spot questions from time to time. They love it; I interview people on the radio all day, so it's small wonder they love to turn the tables on me, too.

Continued overleaf →

Again, interview technique is something that many adults have never been taught. A friend of mine literally talked herself out of a job after being asked what her worst habit was. 'I talk too much! I'd probably talk to the customers all day, I wouldn't be able to stop myself. I'd never get any work done …' She was trying to show that she was an amiable person but it totally backfired.

Ava was recently filmed doing an online interview for the first time, so all our practice came in handy.

Good things to practise for interviews are:

• Before the interview, read through your application, letter, and CV several times to remind yourself of all the reasons you believe you have what they are looking for.

• Keep calm. Yes, this is easier said than done, and people will understand if you are nervous, but staying in control will stop you from getting flustered by a tricky question.

• Take your time. Think about the questions before you answer. One useful tip to buy yourself a few moments and keep your mind focused is to repeat the question in your answer, for example:

  – What are the top three qualities you think you can bring to this role?

  – There are lots of qualities I think I can offer, but the top three I think I would bring to the role are …

• If you're put on the spot, and are not sure of the answer, it's okay to say, 'Can I think about that?' or 'I'd be happy to get back to you about that'.

• Don't be afraid to ask questions about the role or organization. It's a great opportunity to show you have done your research and that you're genuinely interested and keen – and interviews are as much about knowing that this is a good fit for you as the other way round.

• Don't let the pressure of the interview, or a surprising question when you are hoping to get the job, make you agree to something you regret later (e.g. hours, salary, tasks). At the same time, don't close doors either if there is a role you didn't expect, but which you are offered. As my dad used to say, 'Just get in the door!'

Write an invoice

Throughout my career it's always been important to me to know exactly what's coming in and going out of my account – and as I don't have a 'regular' job, making sure I get paid for the work I have done is a big part of that.

It's something I have passed on to my kids, who have to earn their pocket money, but if Ava does a job for me I won't pay her unless she provides a ledger. Why? Because I've got friends who are awful at invoicing and then complain when they haven't been paid. So I say to Ava, 'This is what I need to know from you. Let's see your ledger and find out':

- What job did you do for me?

- How much did you get paid?

- What date did you do the job?

- Did you get my signature?

And then, only then, will I give her the money. The only time she'll get paid is if she can provide written evidence. Of course, I'm in the house. I know she's done the job, so I could just say, 'Thank you for cleaning the windows, here's £2'. But doing it this way means she's thought about it and she has learned the value of her time and her work, as well as an important skill for later life – how to invoice – should she go into a profession that needs it.

After lockdown Ava came to the bank with me and we ticked off every single job: there must have been 200 of them. Some were big jobs. Some were little jobs. But when we added it all up I said, 'How much? Add that up again, it can't be right.' But it was, it was brilliant. And I couldn't argue because she had her ledger to back it all up!

Feel confident about speaking in public

I might have spent a lot of time on stage as an adult, but I was never confident about public speaking when I was younger. One of my school reports said: 'If Myleene's name wasn't on the register we wouldn't know she was in the class at all.' That's always stuck with me and really makes me think what a turnaround I've had.

Reading it back now I feel really sorry for that girl: she was very timid and really toeing the line, with her head down. It wasn't until I started to succeed at what I wanted to do that I started to find some confidence. Before that there was nothing cool about anything I did. I was a total nerd, into classical music. My nerdiest moment: I created a Planets Club that limited its membership to nine (like the planets – Pluto hadn't been relegated at that point). But even then I couldn't find eight others to join me! Not to be defeated, I made a magazine where I wrote facts about planets, drew pictures of planets … If one of my daughters did something like now I'd think it was really brilliant, but it was a running joke in our family for years.

Even when I was in Hear'Say, I still found public speaking hard. There were some very strong personalities among us so it would have been all too easy to stay in the background. It was actually one of the judges from the show who said to me, 'Not everything you say has to be perfect.' That was a real turning point. I'd come from music college and an Asian family background where perfection was key, so that was a revelation for me.

Whether you're addressing a meeting, doing a presentation in class, making a speech at a celebration, or anything else, the principles for successful public speaking are the same. Here's what you need to know to nail that speech.

- It's normal to be nervous. Don't get stressed by the butterflies in your stomach; they happen to the best of us. Deep, slow breaths help.

- If you're not good at being put on the spot or busking it then practise, practise, practise.

When I was at college something else that someone said to me was 'Just take off your make-up.' It took a very long time for me to be able to do that, which sounds ridiculous now because I often go out without make-up, or do FaceTimes or videos, but then it was my war paint, my mask. Taking it off was fundamentally a big deal for me because I was hiding behind it, but by having to be me, to use my voice and actually say something, I realized that making that simple change gave me the confidence to do it.

These days I don't get nervous at all when it comes to speaking or performing, though I do feel the fear when I do something outside my comfort zone – like learning to ice-skate for a TV show. But that was a phenomenal teaching experience and a great reminder that sometimes it's good to push yourself out of your safe little bubble.

- Know your strengths. When Ava had her first interview we asked for the questions in advance so she could go over them and would know what she wanted to say. It worked really well because she felt prepared. I could throw Hero into a room full of people and she'd honestly have them eating out of her hand. She's very reactionary and good at reading people, but by her own admission, if she had gone to the trouble of preparing a dialogue she would probably forget it! They are both very different characters with different strengths, so make sure you recognize yours and play to them.

- Notes. If you can have them, make sure they're in the right order, are easy to read (printed is generally better than handwritten), and give you clear pointers of what you want to say.

- Technology. If you're using PowerPoint or similar, make sure you have a backup version (on a stick or email) just in case.

- Think positive. Visualize yourself delivering your speech exactly how you'd like it to go.

There's an old saying that to avoid being intimidated by your audience you should imagine them naked and/or on the toilet, but this can definitely be more distracting than useful!

Manage a household budget

The concept of budgets can be difficult for children (and adults!) to understand. If I say to the girls, 'Get out of the shower, you're using all the hot water!' or 'Close the window, you're letting all the heat out!' they don't really get it. They don't see the energy they are wasting or feel the money, they just literally think, she's nagging me again.

But one day they're going to need to find somewhere to live, whether they're renting or lucky enough to be able to buy a flat or house. So they're going to have to know how to budget. And the best way to teach them is by turning it into a game.

We use pasta pieces instead of money, as money in its own right can be pretty confusing for young kids. The concept of money is so abstract to children and it's hard for them to really get the difference of £10, £100 and £1,000. But pasta pieces, just by the sheer volume of them, can make a brilliantly visual impact that's perfect for kids and helps them understand that they have a finite amount to 'spend'.

So, I show my girls that different things are worth different amounts and that it's important to make sure you have taken all of those things into account.

You have 100 pieces of pasta (have fun counting those out!) and now you have to work out how best to make them work for your needs.

So, there's:

- **Twenty for tax.**
- **Ten for the mortgage or rent.**
- **Four for the car** – but within that are more costs; insurance, tax, MOT, servicing, and let's not forget fuel.

I get them to name everything that they can – gas, water, electricity, phone, uniform, toiletries, car, fuel – and for each one they have to put more of the pasta pieces into an empty jar. Then there are the 'hidden' costs as well. You might budget for a toothbrush, but that's no good without toothpaste, and so on.

I make sure that at the end they are left with just one piece and I'll say, that is for you. That is for you to go to the cinema, to go and spend on drinks with your friends, picnics, bubble tea. They'll be so happy about it, and then I'll say, My tyre's just burst and make them hand it over!

THE IMPORTANCE OF SAVING

Once you've taught them the idea of budgeting, it makes more sense to them to talk about the concept of saving. It's now much more obvious why I say to them if you want to spend that one piece that's great, but you could put it in the bank, or you could put it away for a rainy day, and then next month you'll have another one.

In our budgeting lesson, I don't want to make it easy, because if it looks like it's easy to save it will be just as easy to spend. So that's why I just leave them with one, sometimes two, pieces of pasta if I'm feeling generous – and the shock on their faces is worth it every time. In fact, now we almost play the game for the shock, even though they know it's coming!

But underneath the fun of the game, the message is important for them. It's true – it's all happened. I've had times where I thought I'd finally got my life on track, I felt really confident and I was back in the black ... and then the roof started to leak and I'd got to find thousands of pounds and pay for the scaffolding and the labour, and I had to do it otherwise the roof's going to cave in. The kids love the drama of these scenarios, but they also understand how budgeting works by the end of each game. Win-win.

5

Rescue remedies

Ava, aged 8, and Hero, aged 5, learning CPR and the recovery position with St John Ambulance

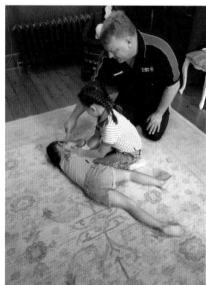

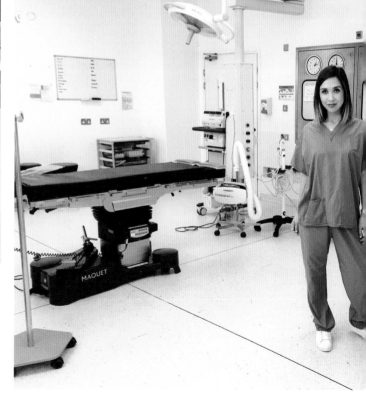

Me working with the NHS

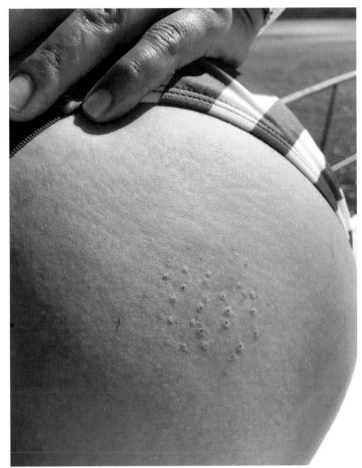

Jellyfish sting in Ibiza.
Use a hotel keycard to
remove the spines

Perform CPR

I haven't ever had to put my CPR skills into practice and, touch wood, I hope it stays that way. But I don't ever, ever, ever want to be in a position where I need to know how to do it and I don't know what to do. That terrifies me.

My biggest fear is something happening to my children. None of them take this into consideration, though, in their day-to-day lives: Hero has always been the most accident-prone person; my heart was always in my mouth when she was younger, and now that she's slowly finding her balance, I've got a toddler who's just started climbing the wine rack. So it starts all over again! But if somebody breaks their arm I know they're not going to die from it; if they can't breathe, though, there is a greater possibility that it won't end well – and that's why CPR is, to me, the most important lesson you can learn.

I think it's an absolute travesty that this simple technique is not just taught in all schools. It's so important. It should be lesson number one. Yes, having to save someone's life is a daunting prospect at any age, but remember that children don't catastrophize or panic unless you present them with a catastrophe or something to panic about. They don't automatically attach emotion to situations unless they have learned to do so from you, so it's all about how you sell it to them. If you can turn a potentially stressful situation, like giving CPR, into a game, you can teach vital practical skills without it being scary for them. Of course, a child cannot sustain CPR on an adult, but they *can* tell another adult how to do it – and that in itself has saved lives on a number of occasions.

WHEN TO PERFORM CPR
You should only perform CPR on someone who is **unresponsive**.
- To determine this, shake the patient by the shoulders and shout loudly: 'Can you hear me? Can you open your eyes? Can you squeeze my hand?'
- If there's no response, get to work as quickly as possible.

BEFORE YOU START
- Shout for help.
- Get someone to call an ambulance while you stay with the patient.
- If there's no one else around, dial 999 before you start giving CPR.

If you're in a public place that is likely to have a defibrillator – such as a leisure centre, shopping centre, or airport – use it. Don't be intimidated; follow the instructions on the device carefully – they are very simple, easy to follow, and clear.

TO START CPR

For adults, unless you've been fully trained and are confident in rescue breaths (see page 100) with CPR, you should only attempt chest compressions.

1   Place the heel of your hand in the centre of the patient's chest. Put your other hand on top and interlock the fingers so that you are using both arms for the compressions.

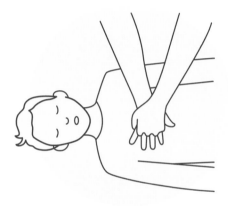

2   Keeping your arms straight, push the breastbone down firmly and smoothly, and then release.

3   Aim for around 100–120 compressions per minute, or around two per second. You can make sure the pace is correct by singing 'Staying Alive' and doing your compressions in time to the beat.

4   It can be exhausting to keep up compressions, so if there's someone else there, take it in turns if it becomes too tiring for one person to continue.

5   Keep going until professional help arrives to take over or until the patient shows signs of regaining consciousness (for example, opening their eyes, trying to speak, coughing, or breathing normally again.)

Since the COVID-19 outbreak, the advice on giving rescue breaths has changed further. Now the recommendation is that it's safest to avoid putting your face close to that of the patient and to find some light material, such as a T-shirt or tea towel, to cover their nose and mouth to prevent droplets reaching you.

Perform CPR on a child

Performing CPR on a child is similar to doing it on an adult, but there are some key differences that are important to know.

WHEN TO PERFORM CPR
Only if the child is unresponsive and has stopped breathing.

BEFORE YOU START
- Shout for help.
- Get someone to call an ambulance while you stay with the patient.
- If there's no one else around, perform CPR for one minute then dial 999 before you continue.

TO START RESCUE BREATHS
Rescue breaths are more important in CPR with kids, as it's more likely that a child has stopped breathing due to a problem with their airways, rather than their heart, especially as the majority of CPR for kids happens as a result of incidents in water. So, to do this:

1   Make sure the child is lying flat on their back.

2   Open their airway by tilting their head back gently, by placing one hand on their forehead and two fingers under their chin.

3   If you can clearly see an obstruction and can remove it safely (with no danger of pushing it further in), do so carefully.

4   Pinch the soft part of their nose, form a seal around their mouth, and give 5 breaths (with a pause between each). You should see their chest rise.

'Rescue breaths are more important in CPR with kids.'

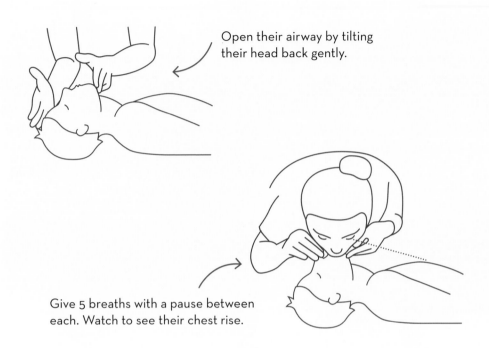

Open their airway by tilting their head back gently.

Give 5 breaths with a pause between each. Watch to see their chest rise.

The rescue breaths should be followed by chest compressions. These are not quite the same as the ones used on adults, so make sure you know the difference:

1   On children you should only use **one hand** to do the compressions.

2   Place the heel of your hand in the centre of the child's chest.

3   Keep your arm straight and press down 30 times – remember 'Staying Alive' or 'Nellie the Elephant' to keep the pace correct. (Again, this can get tiring pretty quickly. If there's someone with you, taking turns will help.)

4   Don't worry about pressing too hard – it's better than not doing it hard enough. It's not unusual for a rib to be broken during CPR, which sounds alarming, but that's definitely preferable to the alternative.

5   After 30 compressions, do 2 more rescue breaths.

6   Repeat this 30:2 ratio until help arrives.

If someone is choking

A couple of years ago we were on holiday. I was relaxed and my defences were down, so when Ava started to choke I didn't immediately realize what was happening. One minute she was eating calamari and chatting, the next she was clutching her throat. I thought she was messing around.

There was a deafening silence and no one moved. I think we were all in shock. But I knew that if I panicked – which is a natural reaction and so easy to do – it could cost vital seconds in saving her life. So the moment I realized she was actually choking I jumped over the table and whacked her three times on the back. She sprang back to life and then carried on eating like nothing had happened. Meanwhile, I sat and sobbed for the rest of the evening, which she thought was hilarious.

It happened to Hero too. When she was about one and a half she came to find me in the kitchen – thank heavens. She was too young to explain what was wrong, although the blockage meant she wouldn't have been able to talk anyway (despite what you often see in films or on TV, when people choke it's usually silent), but she was holding her throat and turning blue. I lay her on her front, angled along my arm, and hit her five times really hard on her back. And nothing happened. I sat her up then put her down again and hit her really hard on the back again. Still nothing. It wasn't until the third attempt that it worked. She was sick, and in among the vomit and the blood was a small plastic star. She walked off happily – and after that I became a maniac with the hoover, always looking for Lego and Barbie shoes!

Thankfully I knew exactly what to do in that moment, but I've made sure that both my girls are now well-versed in how to help someone in the same situation. We used a soft toy as a demonstration model so we could repeat the process until they felt fully confident.

IF A CHILD OR ADULT IS CHOKING:

 use your finger to fish around in their mouth to try to remove the obstruction; you might end up pushing it further down.

 ask them whether they are choking and whether they are able to cough and clear the blockage themselves. If they are not able to do this, here's what you need to do:

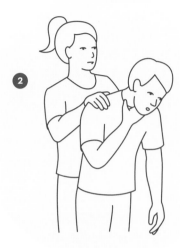

1   Help them to lean forward, then support their upper body. Leaning them over your arm is a good way to do this.

2   Using the heel of your hand, administer 5 sharp blows on their back in between their shoulder blades.

3   If that doesn't work you now need to do 5 abdominal thrusts.

   • Stand behind them and place your hands under their chest, just above the belly button.

   • Clench your fist then wrap your other hand around it.

   • Pull sharply inwards and upwards 5 times.

4   If they haven't coughed up whatever was obstructing their airway, call an ambulance and continue with the blows and the thrusts.

5   If they are unresponsive start CPR (see page 98) while you wait for the ambulance to arrive.

Continued overleaf →

IF A BABY IS CHOKING

For children under one, the technique is slightly different:

1   If you can, sit down and lay your baby face down over your thigh, making sure you support their head.

2   Use the heel of your hand to deliver 5 short, sharp, back blows in between their shoulder blades, each time checking whether the blockage has come out.

3   If this doesn't work, turn the baby onto their back, still making sure that you support their neck and head, and deliver 5 chest thrusts by pressing down hard with 2 fingers.

4   If necessary, follow points 4 and 5 above.

Knowing what to do in this situation really can make the difference between life and death. After working with St John Ambulance, the girls and I made videos of what to do and put them up them on TikTok. Just a day after I posted I received this message:

> *I watched your choking video yesterday ... I've just carried out the abdominal thrusts manoeuvre on my wife who was choking on a piece of chicken. Between you and me we just saved a life. It's scary how quick it happens and in those first few seconds you don't think they are choking. I attended a first-aid course a few years ago but the refresh of watching you and your kids focused the mind. Take a bow, Myleene, and thank you.*

I was blown away by the message. We all scroll through social media absent-mindedly, but the fact that he scrolled, saw the video, and took it in saved a life. Incredible.

LESSONS FOR LIFE

My kids have learned plenty of first-aid techniques, and to them it's a game. It's doctors and nurses. But the point is they KNOW what to do if it's needed, and it really makes a difference. They've helped on three occasions with the skills they've learned, and they were magnificent; once on a plane, once on a train, and once on the street when an old man tripped over his own suitcase crossing the road. I pulled the car over and Hero helped me. She was brilliant. I was so proud. Everything they had learned through what they thought was play came into its own in those moments and gave them the confidence to know how to help.

If someone faints

WHY DO PEOPLE FAINT?

There are lots of reasons, and some are more serious than others; they include shock, being upset or very angry, being too hot, not having eaten or drunk enough water (especially in heat), low blood pressure, heart problems, severe pain, or because of drugs or alcohol.

WHAT ARE THE SYMPTOMS?

They include feeling dizzy and/or sick, sweating or the skin becoming cold or clammy, going pale, and sometimes disturbed vision or slurred speech.

If someone is showing any of the above symptoms, you should:

1   Get them to lie down with their legs raised (which helps the blood flow to the head). If this isn't possible they should sit and lower their head between their knees.

2   Give them water to sip or get them to try to eat something.

3   Loosen any tight clothing.

4   Get them to take deep breaths.

If they do faint:

1   Make space around them and if they don't come round quickly put them into the recovery position (see page 106).

2   If they can't be woken within a minute, are having a fit or seizure, or hurt themselves when they fell, you should call an ambulance.

I once fainted very dramatically when I was in Egypt and someone gave me the wrong meds. I don't remember too much about it, but it's really good to know what to do if it happens to someone else. When a famous pop star fainted near me once, I cleared a space and undid her bra, making sure there was no other tight clothing and that she was comfortable in a clear space. I could see she was about to pass out and asked if she was pregnant, but then down she went before she could answer. She was breathing normally so I put her in the recovery position and she was fine afterwards (and she was pregnant!).

Put someone in the recovery position

I learned this on the course I did with St John Ambulance, little realizing I would need to put it into practice just a couple of days later when an elderly lady passed out on a very hot train. But knowing exactly what to do absolutely gave me the confidence to help her without panicking.

WHEN SHOULD YOU DO THIS?

If someone is unconscious but they are breathing normally, you should put them into the recovery position to make sure that their airway is kept clear and they won't choke if they vomit.

HOW TO DO IT

It's hugely important that **before you do anything** you make sure that the person is not suffering from spinal or other injuries. If they have fallen from a height, are complaining of severe pain in their back or neck, are unable to move their neck, or feel numb or paralysed and can't move their limbs – or if they have lost control of their bowel or bladder – you shouldn't move them, but you can still check that their airway is clear. To do this put your hands on either side of their neck and very gently lift their jaw with your fingertips – but be VERY careful not to move their neck.

It's so easy for panic to take over – somebody falls and everybody starts shouting, 'We need to move them,' 'They've crashed wearing their helmet, we need to take the helmet off.' Take a breath. Panic makes you go against your common sense. The helmet stays in place. Don't move them unless you absolutely have to – for instance, if there is a danger of further injury if you don't.

'Take a breath. Panic makes you go against your common sense.'

TO PUT SOMEONE IN THE RECOVERY POSITION

1 Make sure the person is lying on their back and kneel next to them.

2 Loosen any tight clothing.

3 Straighten their arms and legs, then take the arm nearest to you and extend it at a right angle, with the palm facing up.

4 Then take their other arm and fold it over their body so that the back of the hand rests under the cheek closest to you. When you've done this, keep holding it in place with one hand.

5 Use your free hand to bend the knee farthest from you to a right angle, then pull on the bent knee to roll the person onto their side. The bent arm should support their head and the outstretched one will stop them rolling too far and ending up face-down.

6 Check that the bent leg is still at a right angle when it has folded across the body.

7 Make sure that the airway is open. You can do this by gently tilting the head back and lifting the chin to check that nothing is blocking it.

8 Stay with them, keeping them in this position, until help arrives.

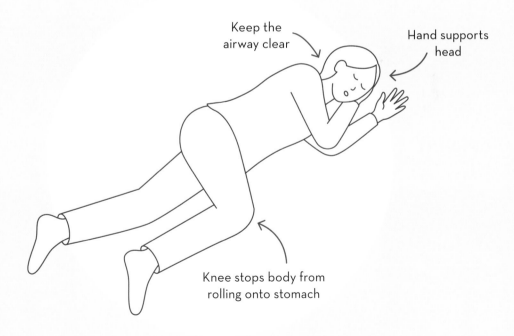

Keep the airway clear

Hand supports head

Knee stops body from rolling onto stomach

Recognize a stroke

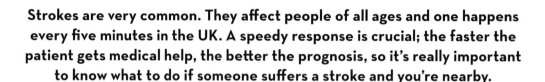

Strokes are very common. They affect people of all ages and one happens every five minutes in the UK. A speedy response is crucial; the faster the patient gets medical help, the better the prognosis, so it's really important to know what to do if someone suffers a stroke and you're nearby.

Identifying what's happening is key. Sometimes people mistake a stroke for drunkenness and think that the person will just sleep it off, but to leave them to it is the worst thing you can do.

The Stroke Association recommends using the FAST technique:

FACE   Ask the person if they are able to smile and check whether their face has fallen on one side.

ARMS   Ask the person whether they can raise both arms and keep them there.

SPEECH   Check whether they can speak clearly and understand what you are saying to them. Note whether their speech is slurred.

TIME   This is crucial, so if you see any of the three things above dial 999 as quickly as possible.

Other symptoms that you should look out for include sudden weakness or numbness on one side of the body (including legs, hands, or feet), difficulty finding words or speaking in clear sentences, sudden blurred vision or loss of sight in one or both eyes, sudden memory loss or confusion, dizziness or a fall, or a sudden, severe headache. Again, call 999 as quickly as you can.

MINI STROKES

A mini stroke (also known as a TIA, or transient ischaemic attack) presents the same symptoms as a full stroke, although it will generally last only for a short time. Even if the symptoms have gone, though, it's still really important to get the patient to hospital as quickly as possible.

About nosebleeds

WHAT CAUSES A NOSEBLEED?

The inner lining of the nose is delicate and damage to it can result in a nosebleed. These can happen:

- When you blow your nose too hard (for example, if you have hay fever or a bad cold).
- When the inside of your nose is too dry (mainly caused by a change in air temperature).
- Because of high blood pressure or an injury/fracture to the nose.
- If certain medicines (such as heparin or warfarin) thin the blood.
- Due to conditions that affect how your blood clots or the blood vessels themselves.

They can also happen because you've been picking your nose too vigorously!

IF YOUR NOSE IS BLEEDING ...

1 **Don't lie down** – make sure you stand or sit in an upright position.

2 **Pinch your nose** just above your nostrils and hold for 10 to 15 minutes.

3 **Lean forward** and breathe through your mouth.

4 **Place an icepack** (or a bag of frozen peas wrapped in a tea towel) at the top of your nose.

5 If the bleeding started after a blow to your head, or it lasts longer than 10 to 15 minutes, is excessively heavy, or you are swallowing a large amount of blood that makes you vomit, feeling weak, or dizzy, or are having difficulty breathing, you should **seek medical attention** as soon as possible.

I suffered so badly from nosebleeds when I was younger and my stepdaughter suffers from them now too, so we are well-versed in what to do. I could actually activate a nosebleed to get out of things I didn't want to do – I just used to tap my nose, it was that sensitive. But it was something that I grew out of. In those days there was all the stuff about holding your head back and now it's about tipping it forward. Everyone's got a technique and it can very easily get a bit old wives' tale-ish, but ultimately it's just pinch and hold, and sit still for 10 minutes.

HOW TO

Make a sling

WHY YOU MIGHT NEED A SLING

If you have injured your upper arm, forearm, or wrist, a sling will provide the necessary support by holding your forearm in a horizontal or raised position. It also shows other people that you have an injury and that they should be careful around you!

What if you don't have a bandage? Slings are generally made from triangular bandages (often a large square that's folded diagonally), but if you don't have one, plenty of other things can be pressed into service until you have something more suitable to hand. You can use a belt, or a tie; a scarf, a cut-up T-shirt or pillowcase would work too. My dad and I used a belt for my younger sister when she fell out of a tree when she was little.

HOW DO YOU TIE A SLING?

When my sister broke her arm, all we ever did was make slings for her for three months, so we all got plenty of practice. It's all about getting the right shape around the elbow and providing the best support. Don't pin it too high – your wrist should be in line with, or slightly higher than your elbow – otherwise that will add more pressure to the injured arm. St John Ambulance, obviously experts in this field, advise:

1   Get the person who has been injured to support their arm with their 'good' hand.

2   Gently slide the bandage underneath the injured arm. The point of the triangle should be beneath the elbow.

3   Bring the top end of the bandage around the back of the neck.

4 Fold the lower end of the bandage up over the forearm to meet the top of the bandage at the shoulder of the injured side.

5 Tie the two ends of the bandage together in a reef knot (see page 259) above the injured person's collarbone, and tuck in the free ends.

6 Adjust the part holding the arm so that it supports it all the way from the elbow to the end of their little finger.

7 Make sure that the edge of the bandage by the elbow is secured by fastening with a safety pin or carefully twisting the fabric and tucking it in.

8 Check the circulation in their fingertips every 10 minutes. You can do this by pressing one of their nails for 5 seconds until it turns pale, then releasing to see if the colour returns within 2 seconds. If it looks as though circulation is impaired, loosen or remove the sling and any underlying bandages, but keep the arm elevated.

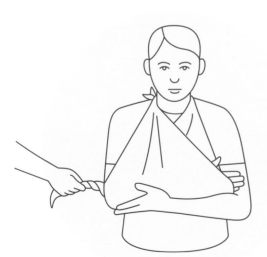

Understanding a first-aid kit

It's a really good idea to have a first-aid kit. I have quite a few – a big one at home and pared-down versions for when I'm out and about or on holiday. But what should be in it? And why?

For me it's about what I might need for splinters (tweezers), or cuts and grazes (saline solution for cleaning, antiseptic cream, and plasters), creams for burns and bites, a bandage. Scissors. Calpol/paracetamol (Calpol all day long!) for temperatures. Freeze gel (thinking of when my partner Sim dislocated his toe when we were in Croatia and I had to pull it out and twist it to get it back. Not fun, but I'd had lots of practice on Ava, whose shoulder regularly used to pop out when she was smaller). If you're going abroad, stuff for dodgy tummies ...

Here's what you should keep in a full first-aid kit – and what you might need the various things for.

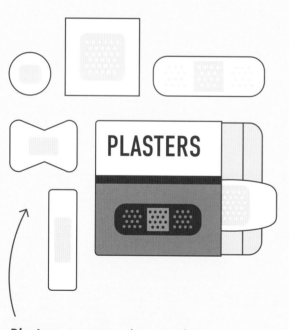

Plasters – in various shapes and sizes. For covering cuts and grazes.

Crepe rolled bandages – great multitaskers. They can be used for keeping dressings in place, or for applying light pressure to a limb or joint to help reduce swelling, provide support, or relieve pain.

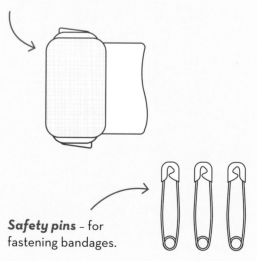

Safety pins – for fastening bandages.

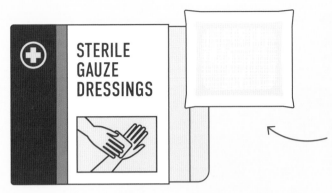

Small, medium, and large sterile gauze dressings – for larger wounds. For either of the above, make sure that the wound and surrounding skin is cleaned properly first. Stop any bleeding by applying pressure and – if possible – raising the affected leg/arm higher than the heart. Choose a dressing that is larger than the wound. And always wash your hands before applying a dressing!

At least two sterile eye dressings – these are used for covering minor eye injuries and help protect against infection. Again, washing hands before dressing is key. BUT – if the eye injury is severe or there's something embedded in the eye, do not use the dressing and seek urgent medical advice.

Triangular bandages – for making slings (see page 110).

Tweezers – great for removing splinters, thorns, cactus spikes, and stings, as well as fragments of glass or plastic, and so on.

Disposable sterile gloves – provide protection against infection when treating wounds, and also help first aiders avoid contact with bodily fluids. Ideally you should choose latex-free gloves, as many people are allergic to latex.

Continued overleaf →

Scissors – used for cutting bandages and gauze.

CLEANSING WIPES

Alcohol-free cleansing wipes – for sanitizing wounds and the skin around them, and for cleaning the first aider's hands when there's nowhere to wash them.

HYDROCORTISONE

Cream for skin rashes – for example, hydrocortisone or calendula. Provides relief from itching and irritation.

Sticky tape – good for securing dressings or for applying extra pressure.

35.5°C

Thermometer – ideally digital. This will identity whether the patient has a fever, which can then be treated with medicine such as paracetamol.

Antiseptic cream – does what it says on the tube.

COUGH MEDICINE

Dry, tickly cough

ANTISEPTIC CREAM

Cough medicine – there are different types of these for dry and chesty coughs. If a cough leaves you short of breath, lasts for more than 3 weeks, is very bad or gets worse quickly, is accompanied by chest pain or a very high fever, you should seek medical attention.

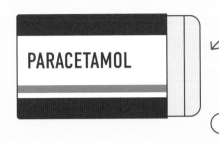

Painkillers – such as paracetamol or ibuprofen (with infant versions for children under 12). Note that aspirin should never be given to children under 16.

Antihistamine cream/tablets – these relieve symptoms of allergies and reactions to bites. Some are also used to treat travel sickness, too.

Distilled water – for cleaning wounds.

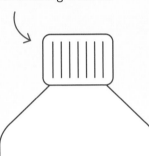

Eye wash and eye bath.

!!!

Note – make sure you regularly check the use-by dates of any medicines in your kit. Always make sure the kit is kept dry and out of the reach of small children.

Treat a jellyfish sting

If you are unlucky enough to get stung by a jellyfish in the sea the best thing to do is find either a lifeguard or someone else who has first-aid training.

But if help isn't available, you should follow these simple steps:

1 Rinse the affected area with sea water (not fresh water).

2 Remove any spines left in the skin – you can use tweezers if you have them, otherwise the edge of a bank card should do the trick. I have actually used my hotel keycard to remove the spines. It works.

3 Soak the area in water that is as hot as can be tolerated for at least 30 minutes. If soaking it isn't possible, use flannels or towels soaked in hot water and replace when they start to cool.

4 Take painkillers such as paracetamol or ibuprofen.

And these are the things you should NOT do:

• Pee on the sting (it's a MYTH!!).

• Apply vinegar, ice, or a cool pack.

• Touch any spines with your bare hands.

• Cover the wound.

A jellyfish sting really is the worst. My daughter (Hero, of course) was swimming in front of me and I suddenly saw an imprint on her skin and all her blood rising up to the surface – and then I saw the jellyfish swim off. The screaming! I couldn't calm her down, it was awful. In Ibiza it happens so often that you can run into any of the restaurants and they've all got a special solution, they're so used to it. But it's pretty nasty and none of us has forgotten the trauma of that one.

If someone's clothes catch fire

If you see someone's clothes catch fire it can be terrifying, but it's important to stay calm.

The advice is simple:

STOP   Don't run. It will make the flames worse.

DROP   Lie on the ground as quickly as you can.

ROLL   Roll in heavy fabric or a fire blanket to smother the flames – though if none is available just rolling on the ground will help.

This is a great technique to teach kids; they have a lot of fun practising (shoving your siblings to the floor in the name of first aid – what's not to like?), but this aside, it's an important thing to learn as it's something that can happen so easily – and so quickly.

I've had to put this into practice twice! Once to a woman at the launch of one of my classical albums just before I was about to perform. There were loads of candles everywhere, and she had extensions and backed into one of the candles. Her hair caught fire instantly. I pushed her to the ground and just rolled on her to put it out. It also happened in a nightclub – to a member of a rival band – because of the same thing, hair extensions. I pushed her onto the floor in the VIP area and rolled her too. So, stop, drop, roll is a very valuable lesson to learn!

HOW TO

Treat burns

There are a lot of old wives' tales when it comes to burns and some of the things they suggest can do far more damage than good. Perhaps the worst one is the suggestion that you should put butter on a burn. As a burn can 'cook' for up to 20 minutes, you'd essentially be frying it rather than making it better. Always, always avoid butter!

THIS IS WHAT YOU SHOULD DO

1   Stop the burning process as quickly as you can by getting away from the heat source. If it's someone else who has been burned, make sure that you don't burn yourself in the process of helping them.

2   If there is anything close to the burn, such as clothing, watches, or jewellery, remove it. But if clothing is stuck to the burned area don't try to peel it off; you could make things worse.

3   Cool the burned area using cool or lukewarm running water.

4   If the burn is on the face or around the eyes, try to keep the patient sitting up as much as possible as this will help to reduce swelling.

5   If it's a bad burn, the patient may well go into shock, which can cause their body temperature to drop. It may seem a bit counterintuitive to think about keeping them warm when you are doing everything you can to cool the burned area, but it's important to do this and ensure their temperature doesn't drop below 35°C.

6   Once the cooling is complete you need to cover the burn to help avoid infection. Cling film is ideal for this (put a layer over the burn itself rather than wrapping it around an entire limb). You could also use a CLEAN clear plastic bag for burns on the hand.

7   If the person is in a lot of pain, give them paracetamol or ibuprofen (always following the directions and age/dosage recommendations on the pack).

For minor burns, the above steps should be all you need, although obviously it's important to keep the burn scrupulously clean until it's fully healed. Throughout this period you should continue to avoid using creams and other greasy substances. Never – however tempting it may be – burst any blisters as this can lead to infection.

For more severe burns, it's important to get medical assistance. Do this if:

- The patient is pregnant.

- The patient is under 5 or over 60.

- They have a medical condition (such as diabetes, heart, lung, or liver disease), or they have a weakened immune system (this includes anyone undergoing chemotherapy).

- They show signs of going into shock (the drop in body temperature can make their skin feel cold and clammy. They may also sweat, feel weak or dizzy, and their breathing may be rapid or shallow).

- There are other injuries in addition to the burn.

- They have also breathed in smoke or fumes.

You should go to A&E if:

- The burns are deep or larger than the patient's hand.

- The skin around the burn is charred or white.

- The burns cause blisters and are on the face, arms, hands, legs, feet, or genitals.

- It's an electrical or chemical burn.

DON'T:

- Soak it.

- Use ice or iced water.

- Use butter or any other greasy/fatty substance (including ice cream) – you're basically basting it and helping it 'cook'.

- Use creams.

- Wrap it up at this stage.

KEEP COOL
In the past when I have burned myself (usually deep-frying turon – Filipino snacks filled with banana – SO good), I have just run the burn under the tap for a few seconds and gone on my merry way. When I did my first-aid course I was shocked to learn that the burning can continue for long after the event. So ALWAYS make sure that the cooling process is done properly – and give it the full 20 minutes.

★ *For advice and training courses from St John Ambulance, please visit www.sja.org.uk*

6

Emergency Exits

Working with the London Air Ambulance and
Dr Simon Walsh, emergency medicine and HEMS
(Helicopter Emergency Medical Service) consultant

Travel safely!
Know your
emergency exits

Staying safe in the sea and on a boat

Travelling can throw up a lot of unexpected situations

In a riptide

I love the sea, so do my girls and we go boarding, swimming. My dad was a Navy frogman, so it's perhaps not surprising that I'm obsessed with diving, too. But after someone very close to me lost her brother-in-law to a riptide, the dangers of this occurence are something I have talked to my children about again and again. And if you enjoy surfing or sailing, or just like swimming in the sea, it's essential to know how to react if you get caught in a riptide.

WHAT IS A RIPTIDE?

A riptide will basically pull any object – or person – away from the shore and out to sea, fast. Essentially, it is a powerful current caused by waves breaking on shallow sandbars (submerged or partly exposed ridges of sand that are built up by tides and waves) and then pushing water back out to sea through deeper channels. The sight of sandbars can be deceptive and make it look – to anyone with an untrained eye – as though it's a calmer place to enter the water. But it's not.

HOW TO SPOT A RIPTIDE

Riptides are not obvious, so before you enter the water, have a good look for signs. Look out for:

Possible escape

- Darker patches in the water beside shallower sandbars.

- Rippled or churned water where there are no breaking waves.

- The formation of foam.

- Bits of debris floating out to sea.

- Brown discoloured water where the sand beneath has been disturbed.

- To be absolutely sure you are safe, always swim on lifeguarded beaches and stay between the flags, which mark the safest place to swim based on the conditions at the time.

If you get caught up in a riptide, you will feel a strong current pulling you out to sea. Don't panic, though, stay calm, and:

- Alert others. If you are struggling in a riptide you should raise your hand and shout for help. This applies even if you think you will be able to get out of it: it's always good to have people on hand just in case.

- Keep hold of anything that floats – a bodyboard, a surfboard, a buoy, or a lifebelt.

Continued overleaf →

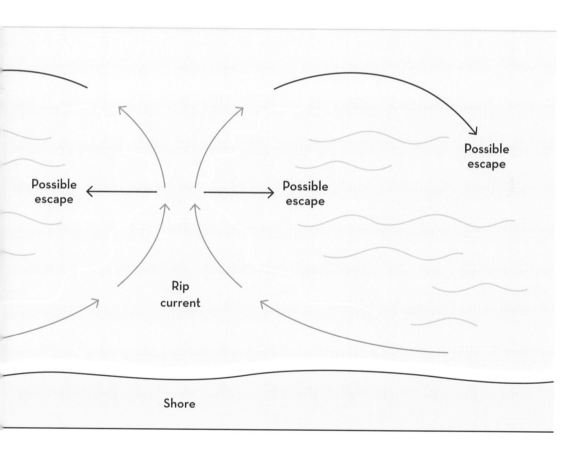

- If there's nothing to hand, flip onto your back, which makes floating much easier (and uses less energy).

- Don't exhaust yourself. Stay calm and try to float to assess the situation. Trying to swim against the force of a rip will use up your energy very quickly and make you more likely to panic. Remember that most people don't die because of the riptide itself but from exhaustion trying to fight against it.

- Work out how deep the water is. If you can stand, wade out of the rip – don't try to swim. These currents can flow at 4–5mph – faster than an Olympic swimmer.

- Swim parallel to the shore if the water is too deep for you to stand. Swim across the direction of the current and use any breaking waves to help you get back to land.

RIDE WITH IT

Remember that a riptide can pull you under the water. If this happens, don't try to swim to the surface (which is what people will often tell you to do) because you won't know where the surface is. I've demonstrated this technique to the girls using a ball. Waves don't go up and down, they go over and around and if you drop the ball into the ocean it will go round in circles, coming to the surface and then going down again. So let the wave take you and you will come back up again and then you're not wasting valuable energy trying to push yourself in the wrong direction.

In a house fire

Long ago I had the chance to go to sea with my dad. I used to hate the fire musters that he'd call on the ship at 4 or 6 a.m. 'You've got to be joking!' I'd complain, but he was absolutely right – fire doesn't always happen at midday after you've had a cup of tea and you're ready for it.

It's only now I really understand the responsibility he would have had as the captain. When you're the parent in the house, you are the captain of that ship and if there's a fire, your job is to make sure everybody knows their routes out and to keep everyone safe.

When talking about dealing with fires on social media, I've had people say, 'You shouldn't be frightening children!' My response is simple: I'd rather empower my kids than put them in a situation where they don't know what to do. It might be scary to discuss for the first time, but not as scary as not having a clue what to do if they find themselves trapped in a house fire. Hero went to nursery with a little boy who got caught in a house fire. When he came back to school they had a little chat about it in her class. The kids have never forgotten these important lessons.

When I put the videos of our drills up on TikTok one woman messaged me to say that when she was a little girl her mum put her sister's bra in the tumble dryer and the metal got caught and started a fire in the middle of the night. Well, that's it! I don't run the dryer at night or when I'm out now because of her story.

Continued overleaf →

**So we have fire drills once a month at home.
I have taught my kids these golden rules:**

GET OUT – DON'T HIDE

It might be a scary situation, but however tempting it is
to hide under a bed or in a cupboard you mustn't do it.
This will make it much harder for parents (or firefighters)
to find and help you.

PLAN DIFFERENT EXITS

It might not be possible to leave by the front door so practise using windows and back
doors too.

AVOID HOT DOORS

Touch a door gently to see if it's hot before you try to open it. Heat means there could
be a fire behind it – and if so, you should try a different route.

KNOW WHO YOU NEED TO HELP OR WHO IS GOING TO HELP YOU

If there are young children, elderly people, or those with limited mobility in the house,
have a plan for a specific person to help them escape and make it clear to everyone else
in the house that in the event of an emergency these people will need help. My kids know
to help the younger ones, and we all know that if the situation arose, whoever is nearest
the person who needs help at the time should take that responsibiity.

REMEMBER THAT SMOKE RISES
This can make it impossible to see where you're going. We have turned this into a learning game and we practise making our way through smoke by wearing blindfolds and staying low.

SMOKE AND GASES CAN BE MORE HARMFUL THAN FLAMES
You need to get out as quickly as possible even if you can't see the fire itself.

NEVER GO BACK FOR TOYS OR PETS

HEAD FOR AN AGREED MEETING OR MUSTER POINT
Once you're out of a burning building, never go back inside.

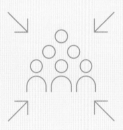

FEEL THE FEAR – AND DO IT ANYWAY
Fire can, of course, be terrifying for children, but rather than selling the fear of something it's important to empower them, to teach them about calculated risk – otherwise you'd never do anything. You'd never go swimming in the sea because you might get eaten by a shark or caught in a riptide. You'd never cross a road because you might get hit by a car. I remember when I was in Australia I'd read about spiders in cars and panicked that I'd get bitten and drive off the road …

So you tell them that fire is amazing; it keeps us warm, it cooks our food, it's given us many incredible opportunities – from being able to create and build things to using it to smelt things down – but we also know that if we touch it we can hurt ourselves badly. And although it's useful, we have to make sure we can control it. That's how you sell it to your children – I've done the same with water (don't stick your head in it) and plug sockets (don't stick your fingers in them).

Life is a never-ending series of calculated risks.

If you smell gas

Knowing what to do when there's a gas leak can save a property from destruction – and people's lives.

IF YOU SMELL GAS INSIDE A PROPERTY

DO

- Call your National Gas Emergency Service number (that's 0800 111 999 in the UK) to notify them of the problem. They will provide advice on what to do next. But before that, you should:

- Open doors and windows to ventilate the property.

- Turn off the gas at the mains tap. This is usually located near the gas meter and has a handle that can be turned 90 degrees. (Note: if the gas leak is in a cellar or basement, do not enter and instead evacuate the building.)

- Always wait for the go-ahead from the gas engineer before re-entering the building.

DON'T

- Turn any power or light switches on or off. (This is common sense, really, but a point I have emphasized to my girls. I still remember the really scary advert from the Eighties saying: 'Don't hit the switch'!)

- Light any sort of flame within the property.

- Use your mobile indoors, as this could cause a spark.

IF YOU SMELL GAS OUTSIDE YOU SHOULD:

1   Call the National Gas Emergency Service (as above) as quickly as possible.

2   Make sure that no naked flames are lit in the vicinity.

3   Wait for an emergency gas engineer to attend and investigate the problem.

If a frying pan catches fire

Many of us remember being told to throw a damp tea towel over a burning pan. There were even public information films made about it. But times have changed, and more recent advice says this a very bad thing to do. So what should you do if you are merrily frying one minute and the whole thing goes whoosh the next?

THIS IS WHAT THE EXPERTS SAY

1   Firstly, never leave a pan unattended – hot oil can set alight quickly.

2   Make sure you don't leave tea towels, aprons, or anything flammable close to the heat (even when it's switched off). They can catch fire easily and it doesn't take much for the flames to spread. The same goes for loose clothing and sleeves.

3   If the pan catches fire, DON'T throw water over it.

4   DO turn off the heat if it is safe to do so.

5   DON'T try to tackle the fire yourself unless you have a proper fire extinguisher to hand.

6   Get out. Stay out. And call the fire service.

'I've set a pan on fire on more than one occasion; I remember my mum doing it too and my dad running in with the tea towel. So it's useful to know that the advice is now to get out as fast as possible and leave the tea towels where they are!'

HOW TO

Call the emergency services

We all know that when there's an emergency we should dial the emergency services (999 in the UK) as fast as we can, but when you're in a state (as many people are – understandably – when they are reporting a fire or an accident or a crime), it's useful to know what happens when you actually make that call. It's a process that's more complex than just dialling the number and someone saying, 'I'll get someone over to you right away', so it can be reassuring to know what you might expect to be asked at each stage and for the different services – police, fire, or ambulance.

1   When you call, the person who first answers will be an operator. They will ask you which service you need: police, fire, or ambulance.

2   If you ask for medical help you will be put through to your local ambulance service. You will be asked for information about what's happened and the patient's condition, and be given advice on what to do until the paramedics arrive. At the end of the assessment, your call will be given a category based on the details you have given.

3   If you ask for the police or fire service you will be asked for details of what the emergency is, and exactly where it is taking place. It's important to try to give information that is as accurate as possible, which will help the operator to assess the level of urgency and priority of the situation, and what help is needed. You will also be asked for your own personal details.

4   When going away, make a note of the local emergency number. Your defences are down on holiday. Most accidents happen at the pool or in a new environment, so be prepared.

WHAT IF I'M IN DANGER AND IT'S DIFFICULT TO SPEAK?

Try to speak if at all possible, even if you can only whisper. The operator might also ask you to cough or to answer questions by tapping keys on your phone.

If you're calling from a landline:

If the operator can only hear background noise and you don't speak or answer questions, they will transfer your call to the police. The police will automatically get information about where you're calling from, and if you hang up the call may remain connected for 45 seconds in case you need to pick it up again.

If you're calling from a mobile:

In the UK, if you are not able to speak or answer questions, the operator will prompt you to press 55 and then your call will be transferred to the police. If you don't press 55, the operator will hang up.

> **Note –** *this doesn't work on a landline and police can't use your number to track your location.*

If you aren't sure where you are, there's a brilliant smartphone app called What Three Words, which gives every 3-metre square of the world a unique combination of three words. If you're in Leicester Square, for example, it will come up with reds.whips.glee to pinpoint your exact location. Many emergency services throughout the world are using this service, but it always helps to have street names to hand, too.

7

Out & about

In the desert. We always learn a few local phrases when we visit different countries

In our local park: Ava, aged 7, and Hero, aged 4. We always have a muster point just in case we lose each other

Ava, aged 2, taking the wheel with me

What would you do if faced with a wild animal? Hero aged 4, and Ava aged 7

Hero, aged 5. What to do when you're lost

Travelling in the cockpit of a light
aircraft over my hometown of Norfolk

Wildlife encounter
in Thailand

My dad was
a Navy diver,
so diving is in
the genes

Swimming with Hero, who could swim before
she could walk — an important life skill

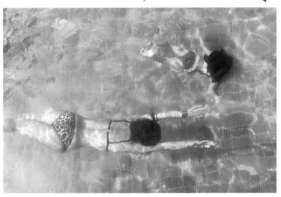

Ava and Hero, aged 7 and 4,
wild swimming in Sweden

HOW TO

Say hello (and more)
in different languages

Yes, the shrug of the shoulders is the universal language for 'I haven't got a clue what you're saying', but showing a bit of effort is so much better than a blank stare or staying silent. It will always help to get people on side if you know even one or two words in their language.

When you're in another country, or speaking to someone whose first language isn't English, I think it's massively important to at least give it a try. You don't have to be able to discuss world politics, even just 'hello', 'thank you', or 'I don't understand' are really good.

If you're going abroad it's quick and easy to learn a couple of phrases – whether it's from a book, a class, an app, or an online course. Being able to communicate is so important. I once worked in a Japanese bar where I picked up a few sentences. A long time later, when I had to interview a Japanese director, the fact I could say hello and introduce myself made all the difference.

There are 6,500 languages used around the world, but the most commonly spoken ones (other than English) are:

	HELLO	GOODBYE	THANK YOU
1. Mandarin Chinese	Nǐ Hǎo	Zài jiàn	Xiè xiè
2. Hindi	Namaste	Namaste	Dhanyavadh
3. Spanish	Hola	Adiós	Gracias
4. French	Bonjour	Au revoir	Merci
5. Arabic	Marhaba	Ma'a as-salaama	Shukran lak
6. Bangla/Bengali	Hello	Bee-daay	Dhonno-baad
7. Russian	Zdravstvuyte	Do svidaniya	Spasibo
8. Portuguese	Olá	Adeus	Obrigada
9. Urdu	As-Salamu-Alaykum	Khuda hafiz	Shukriya
10. German	Guten Tag	Auf Wiedersehen	Danke

And let's throw in the top five in Europe not included above for a nice round (okay, not round at all) 15:

	HELLO	GOODBYE	THANK YOU
11. Turkish	Merhaba	Görüşürüz	Teşekkürler
12. Italian	Ciao	Arrivederci	Grazie
13. Ukrainian	Pryvit	Do pobachennya	Dyakuyu
14. Polish	Dzień dobry	Do widzenia	Dziękuję
15. Dutch	Goedendag	Tot ziens	Bedankt

And, as I'm half Filipina, I absolutely can't forget:

	HELLO	GOODBYE	THANK YOU
16. Tagalog	Kumusta	Paalam	Salamat po

If you are lost

I got lost as a child and it's the worst feeling. Just terrifying. Total panic. And I've lost my kids, too, or at least I thought they were lost because they'd decided to play hide and seek in a shop. Definitely not funny.

So now, whenever we go out, I insist on a muster point. Sim laughs at me, but it works and now everyone appreciates it. And so they should. This is something that's good to have up your sleeve at any age, especially if you're somewhere unfamiliar (such as being on holiday) or busy (like a festival).

If we go on a walk I will find a point and make sure everyone knows that if they lose the rest of us, this is where we will meet up.

RULES FOR A GOOD MUSTER POINT
- Make sure it's somewhere that is easy to find from any point on your route.
- Make sure it's somewhere safe.
- Make sure everyone knows where it is! It defeats the whole object if you all head for different places!

HELPING KIDS HANDLE GETTING LOST
Another thing I have told the kids is that if they can't find us they should go to someone who has children and ask them for help.

With the 2-year-old, who's too young for this yet, I make sure he's always in sight wherever we go. And when he's old enough, I'll do with him what I did with the girls:

1   As soon as possible, make sure they can say their own name.

2   Make sure they know your name ('Mummy' doesn't narrow it down so well).

3   If you're going to be somewhere busy, pop a bracelet onto their wrist with your phone number on it.

Read a map

One of my strongest memories of childhood holidays was when we went on a road trip round Europe. My mum was doing the map-reading and she was meant to follow the blue line. Sounds simple enough, right?

Well, she was wearing sunglasses with yellow lenses so she thought that line was green and followed another one instead. It was horrific. Three kids crammed in the back of the car and miles from where we were supposed to be. So that's when I learned to read maps!

Map-reading is a great skill to have, even in this technological day and age. A proper map gives you so much information and an accurate picture of an area from above. If you can decipher it without having to turn it upside down and wonder what all the squiggles mean, so much the better!

These are the main things you should know:

- Scale matters! It's impossible to get an idea of how near (or far) things are from one another until you know what the scale of the map is. If it's marked 1:50 000 for example, it means that every 1 centimetre on the map represents 50,000 centimetres (or 500 metres) on the ground.

- You can calculate longer distances between two points in a straight line – or as the crow flies – but for shorter distances this will give you a less accurate idea of how long it might take to get somewhere as there may well be buildings/roads/rivers and various other obstructions in your path, meaning you'll need to take a more roundabout route.

- A simple way to measure shorter distances is by using a piece of string. Hold one end at your starting point and lay the rest along the route you plan to take. Mark the string at your finishing point, pull it straight and measure from there to the end you started with. Then use the scale bar to calculate exactly how far that distance is.

- Contour lines will show you how steep/high any hills are; the closer the lines are together, the steeper the incline. On a 1:50,000 map contour lines are marked at 10-metre intervals. Spot heights (a number next to a dot) show specific heights, often at a hill summit or a point of interest. *Continued overleaf →*

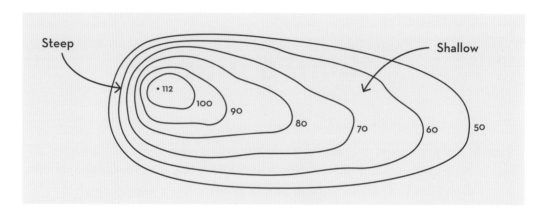

Steep   Shallow

• 112   100   90   80   70   60   50

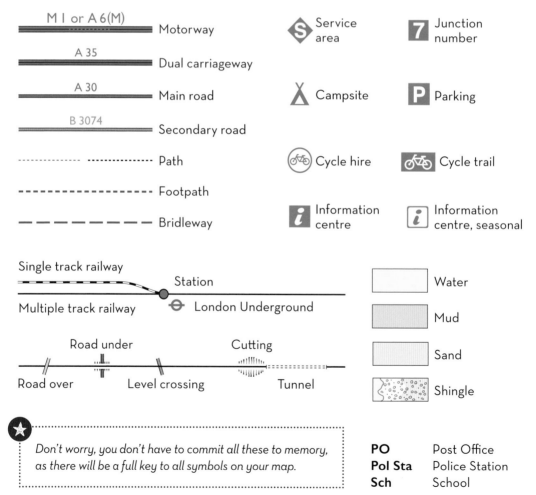

M 1 or A 6(M) — Motorway

A 35 — Dual carriageway

A 30 — Main road

B 3074 — Secondary road

············· ············· Path

-------------------- Footpath

— — — — — — — Bridleway

S Service area

X Campsite

(bike) Cycle hire

i Information centre

7 Junction number

P Parking

(bike) Cycle trail

i Information centre, seasonal

Single track railway

Station

Multiple track railway   ⊖ London Underground

Road over   Road under   Level crossing   Cutting   Tunnel

Water

Mud

Sand

Shingle

★ *Don't worry, you don't have to commit all these to memory, as there will be a full key to all symbols on your map.*

PO   Post Office
Pol Sta   Police Station
Sch   School

- All Ordnance Survey maps have a grid format and use four- or six-figure references to pinpoint specific locations. The first two (or three) of these figures correspond to the vertical lines (also called eastings) and the second two (or three) to the horizontal (known as northings). Six-figure references are accurate to within 100 metres.

- Which way is up? If you are using an OS map then the top is always facing north.

- Symbols are used to represent features on the map – they can be lines (for roads or railways, etc.), small pictures (buildings and more), coloured areas, or letters.

I think knowing how to find your way around places is hugely important (at any age). There have been many occasions when I have said to the kids, 'Right, we need to get here. You lead the way.' It's great practice for them in terms of understanding how to use tubes and trains and working out directions and distance, as they can be pretty confusing at times even, for adults. The lesson here is to teach kids to think for themselves, so they can navigate their way out of a problem if things don't go according to plan (replacement bus services, delays, diversions, etc.). Maps can look very different so this also helps them get accustomed to various layouts.

At the airport I'll also ask them to get us from the departure lounge to the gate. They have to read the ticket and the screens and go through a series of events to get us there – but it's all brilliant learning for the day when they will do this on their own. I'll always guide them if they need it, because it's easy to make mistakes (and obviously catching the plane is the key thing here), but I'm always amazed by how many adults struggle with this so I want them to know what they're doing and feel confident in what can feel like a chaotic airport environment.

SAT NAVS – MAPS FOR A MODERN ERA
In many ways technology has made things a whole lot easier in myriad everyday scenarios. Google Maps and Waze can now help us get from A to B at the press of a button or two. But there's still plenty of room for user error. It's hard to forget newspaper stories of a school trip from Kent to Hampton Court when the coach driver ended up in a north London alleyway with the same name, rather than the Tudor Palace 19 miles to the south-west. I've done the same thing myself; I remember putting in 'Mornington Crescent' and not realizing there are dozens of them all over the country. So the most important thing I have taught the kids is never forget the postcode when you're loading up the sat nav – there might be fifty streets with the same name, so always check you've got the right one before you set off.

Read a world map

There's much more to reading a map than simply finding your way from one place to another. Yes, an A–Z might make all the difference when it comes to navigating your way across a city (who am I kidding? Google maps all the way these days). Though if you're out hiking, then being able to understand scales and symbols is invaluable if you want to get from A to B without ending up lost in a field and having to dig into the emergency bar of Kendal Mint Cake. But when it comes to large-scale maps it's a whole other story.

At school I was a fairly diligent student of geography (as I might have mentioned before, I was a geek long before it was cool), and it's fair to say that I knew my way around an atlas. I could pinpoint Andorra, nestled in the Pyrenees between France and Spain. I could tell you exactly where Sierra Leone was on Africa's west coast (above Liberia and below and to the left of Guinea, in case you were wondering), and that Suriname was the smallest country in South America. In short, I was no stranger to a world map. But what I didn't know until very recently was that when it comes to country sizes, the maps I have been familiar with my whole life are oh, so wrong.

HOW A WORLD MAP WORKS

The world is round and three-dimensional and a map is flat and two-dimensional – and that's where it all gets a bit tricky. Essentially, there's no way of representing every country, continent, or geographical feature accurately and getting it all on one page.

When you 'flatten' the globe everything that gets pushed out towards the top or bottom (or the North/South Poles) will appear bigger and everything around the middle – or the Equator – will look smaller in comparison. (Try making patterns on a sphere of icing and then squashing it – not only will you see how it works but it's also immensely satisfying.)

World maps are nothing new: the first one (based on the fact that the earth was spherical) was drawn up by Eratosthenes in 220 BC. He gained plaudits for the fact that he invented the system of latitude and longitude, but got minus points for the fact he put it together almost 17 centuries before America was discovered, so it was somewhat limited in terms of what it covered (basically Europe, with bits of Asia and Africa).

The world map as most of us know it was drawn up in 1569 by Gerardus Mercator, a Flemish cartographer. But although his version remains a world standard to this day – and is invaluable when it comes to nautical navigation – it has led many of us, me included, to have some fairly distorted ideas about country size.

Go and get an atlas, then take a look at Greenland. Huge, right? About the same size as South America without the tail.

WRONG.

In fact, Greenland would cover just 12 per cent of South America. If you were to actually put one on top of the other, Greenland would only take up a corner of Brazil.

Likewise, Russia looks like it completely dwarfs China on the map, but it's actually 56 per cent of the size.

They don't teach this at school! The Mercator projection is still holding its own, even after almost 500 years. But understanding the real proportions blew my mind the first time I saw maps like this – and I haven't stopped exploring ever since.

THE *ACTUAL* SIZES OF COUNTRIES

Greenland – 2.16 million km²	Australia – 7.692 million km²
Brazil – 8.516 million km²	Canada – 9.985 million km²
Russia – 17.13 million km²	UK – 242,495 km²
China – 9.597 million km²	India – 3.287 million km²

Cope with animal attacks

Even the friendliest of animals can be a hazard when you are out with small children. Imagine being a toddler and seeing a huge dog bounding towards you – it's the equivalent of being charged by a horse as an adult.

It's hard because a perfectly lovely dog might get overexcited and jump at you. As an adult that's one thing, but when you're tiny that can easily knock you flying and be pretty terrifying – and you don't want a single episode to make your child terrified of all dogs, which then becomes a self-perpetuating problem.

As soon my children were old enough I taught them to ask, 'Is your dog friendly? Can I pet your dog?' before they go near any animal they don't know. But I have found myself in a really frightening situation where somebody lost control of their dog. I saw it heading right for Ava, who was strapped in her car seat while I was trying to put her into the car. The dog jumped right into the car with us! I lay on top of Ava so that the dog was on my back. She was safe, but it was pretty scary. It's definitely good to know what to do in these situations, as they can be really dangerous and panicking can make things worse.

- Stay calm. I know this sounds counterintuitive and the likelihood is that it's the opposite to how you'll be feeling inside. But if you show your fear or panic it can aggravate the dog even further.

- If you can, back away slowly. Don't turn your back and run – you don't want the dog to think it's a game of chase. Otherwise, keep still.

- Don't make eye contact or smile. The dog might interpret this as a sign of aggression, which could inflame the situation further.

- The same goes for yelling or screaming. They are obvious things to do but they can make the situation worse. Try to speak to the dog in a low and calm voice, which will have a more soothing effect.

- If you have a bag or coat with you, place it between you and the dog. That way if the dog lunges that's the thing it's likely to make contact with first.

- If you are on the ground, curl into a ball and use your arms to protect your face and keep your fingers curled in a fist. If you are with a small child, curl yourself around them to protect them.

- If you are bitten and the dog doesn't let go, don't pull away – this is likely to provoke a tug of war and make the dog more determined to carry on. Instead, move your limb towards the dog's mouth, which will help prevent further tissue damage.

If you're fond of walking in the countryside there are other animals you might encounter.

SHEEP
Sheep are generally fairly docile, but an angry ram is something you should definitely avoid. The most important thing is to try to demonstrate that you mean no danger. As with dogs, this means staying calm and backing away slowly, without turning your back on it.

COWS
Cows can be dangerous. Although most fatal attacks (in the UK there were 74 between 2000 and 2017) by cows are on farm workers, up to a quarter were on walkers, so it's wise to know what to do (and not to do) if you find yourself in close proximity. Don't forget – the cows are the ones with size on their side.

Most attacks take place when cows have calves with them, because they're in protection mode, so you should avoid entering a field with cows and calves wherever possible. Dogs can also be a factor – the cows can perceive them as a threat, so keep them on a lead, though the advice is that if you are under attack you should let the dog go rather than hold on to it. Stay calm and walk at a steady pace. Running and making loud noises can not only put you at risk, but can also lead to you being prosecuted for worrying the livestock.

Remember, attacks by animals are relatively rare and there are other animals that are much more likely to cause harm, although not necessarily on a ramble in the British countryside. Did you know that the deadliest land mammal is the hippo, which kills more than 500 people a year in Africa? Or that freshwater snails are the cause of more than 20,000 deaths a year (albeit by spreading a disease called schistosomiasis rather than attacking people) – while crocodiles kill around 1,000?

Water-
works

Me, aged 4, on
one of my dad's
working ships

Always at home around water.
Ava and Hero, aged 7 and 4

Going underground.
My job takes me to some
fascinating places

Turn off mains water

Water is pouring through the ceiling. You have three options:

1   Less constructive – panic.

2   More constructive – find a bucket.

3   Most constructive – turn the water off at the mains.

This is easy enough as long as you know where your stopcock is. You'll generally find it under the kitchen sink, but it could also be in an airing cupboard, garage, utility room or cellar, or even under the floorboards near the front door.

If you don't know where yours is, it's a good idea to put this book down and find out straight away! Your best bet is to look close to where the mains water supply enters the property.

TO TURN IT OFF

1   Close the valve by turning it in a clockwise direction. It's not an instant solution: any water already in the system may still drain out, but it's definitely a good idea for damage limitation. When that's gone the water should stop altogether.

2   To turn the water back on, turn the valve the opposite way (anticlockwise). It might take a few minutes for the water to work its way through the system and start running from your taps, so be patient.

3   Most importantly, always turn the stopcock on and off slowly, and don't force it.

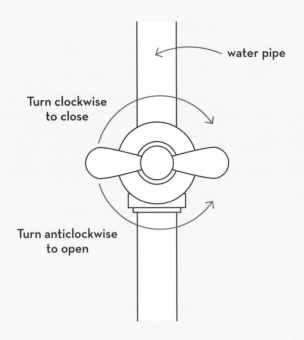

water pipe

Turn clockwise
to close

Turn anticlockwise
to open

'I learned this lesson (the hard way) when the
kitchen was flooding and I didn't know what
to do about it, so I made sure that I found out
where our stopcock was as soon as I moved
into my new house.'

!!!

Another good reason to know where your mains water comes from is in case of a fire.
Firefighters need water quickly to put out the blaze, and connecting to the mains is
the fastest and easiest way of doing it. When this happened to someone I know who
had no idea where their mains tap was, firefighters were forced to use their pond
instead and the whole house stank of stagnant murky water for months.

Unblock a basin/sink

I've lost count of the number of times I've had to do this – usually because of slime being shoved down them (looking at you, girls), which has also ruined my carpets and so has now been banned from the house altogether.

Tip – When you're getting down and dirty with a blocked drain, try to distract yourself with happy thoughts. This will help take your mind off whatever is causing the problem. Hair clumps, rancid food, and fat balls are not for the faint-hearted.

When you need to unclog the bath or the sink, try using one of the following:

1   **A PLUNGER**
    Ideally a flat-bottomed one, but otherwise your common or garden toilet plunger should do the trick. Half-fill the sink with hot water. Put the plunger over the drain and pump it up and down quickly several times. Repeat as needed. I'm a big fan of the plunger and this is definitely my preferred technique.

2   **BOILING WATER**
    Works wonders on clogs caused by soap and shampoo, as well as grease and hairballs (nice). Pour 2 litres of water from a freshly boiled kettle directly into the drain opening then turn on the hot tap. If the water doesn't drain away steadily, repeat. Definitely DON'T try this if your drain is attached to PVC pipes, though, as they may melt.

3   **BICARBONATE OF SODA**
    Scoop out any water remaining in the sink/bath using a small cup then pour a cup of bicarbonate of soda into the drain – use a spoon to push it in if needed. Follow up with an equal amount of white or apple cider vinegar. The reaction will be familiar to anyone whose child has had to make an erupting volcano for school (although this time you can skip the red food colouring bit). When the bubbles subside, put the plug in and wait for 15 minutes. Repeat as needed.

4 BRING OUT THE SNAKE

If all else has failed, a plumber's snake may be the answer to pull out any debris or dislodge any clogs. That said, this probably isn't something that most of us have to hand, so a low-tech version can be pressed into action instead. Use pliers to unbend a wire coat hanger into one long strip (readers of a certain age may have perfected this technique as a child when making a Blue Peter advent crown). Keep a bit of a hook on the end as it comes in handy for nabbing whatever nasties are clogging up the pipe. Feed it slowly down the drain – you don't want to push any obstruction further into the system. Use the hook to snare the debris and carefully pull it back up again. It's a bit like fishing (without the fish, hopefully!).

'Try to distract yourself with happy thoughts!'

If the blockage is in your sink trap (the curved, bending pipe that you can see underneath your sink) rather than the plug hole, you can try checking it for any gunk. This is messy – but effective.

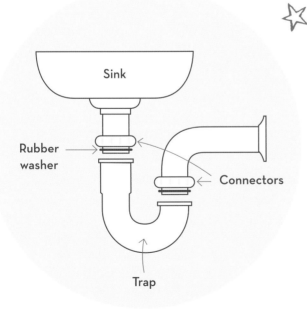

1 Put a bucket or large bowl under the trap.

2 Unscrew the connectors that hold the u-bend onto the vertical and horizontal pipes.

3 Remove and clean out the trap.

4 DO NOT empty everything from the bucket into the sink until you have reconnected the trap (I say this from bitter experience).

5 Put everything back together but make sure you don't over-tighten the connectors as this may cause them to crack.

Unblock a loo

**You flush. You wait. And whatever is in there doesn't disappear.
Or, worse, the water starts to rise ever closer to the top of the toilet bowl.**

The causes of a blocked toilet are many and varied: too much paper, wet wipes or sanitary products (bin them instead), toys, goldfish (don't ask), or what's euphemistically known as 'waste'. It sounds obvious not to drop things into the loo that might cause a blockage, but who hasn't left their phone in their back pocket and then had to gingerly reach into the bowl to fish it out? Or found a toddler experimenting with which toys float and which sink? These things happen.

HERE'S HOW TO DEAL WITH IT

1   If the water's draining away, even if it's very slowly, try flushing again to see if that shifts the blockage. If the water continues to rise, introducing more water is only going to get messy, so stop flushing!

2   Try flushing it out with hot water and washing-up liquid. Close the water supply valve on the cistern (this is usually behind the loo), then scoop as much water as possible out of the bowl. It's definitely a good idea to wear gloves for this bit! Pour 100ml washing-up liquid into the toilet bowl and leave it for 10 minutes. Then add 2–3 litres of hot water (not boiling – cracking the porcelain is definitely not going to help). The water level should fall after a few minutes. Once it's working again, turn the water valve back on. And if all else fails, it's on to ...

3   ... the plunger. Cover the outlet from the bowl and pump – gently at first but then with more force until the water starts to recede.

4   The bad news is that plungers aren't so good on, ahem, solid waste. That needs dissolving, so it's back to our old friend bicarbonate of soda. Pour half a cupful into the toilet. Heat 2–3 litres of water in a saucepan then add half a cup of white vinegar. Leave to cool slightly (you don't want to crack the porcelain!), then pour this mixture into the toilet bowl.

5   Try the snake/coat hanger. Feed it gently into the waste pipe coming from the toilet bowl, hook first, until you can feel the blockage, then rotate to break it up until it can be hooked up or flushed down.

6 If all else fails, try a chemical product – just follow the instructions on the packet.

> *I first learned the coat-hanger trick from an air hostess. I went to the toilet and discovered it was blocked so she offered to get me a hanger to sort it out (thanks). But there was no way I was messing around with whatever was down there in mid-air so I said I'd sit that one out thank you, and found another loo.*

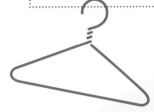

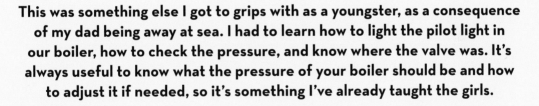

HOW TO
Check the pressure on a boiler

This was something else I got to grips with as a youngster, as a consequence of my dad being away at sea. I had to learn how to light the pilot light in our boiler, how to check the pressure, and know where the valve was. It's always useful to know what the pressure of your boiler should be and how to adjust it if needed, so it's something I've already taught the girls.

What/where is the pressure gauge? It's usually on the front of your boiler; it shows the pressure (no great shock there) of the hot water running through your heating system.

What's the correct pressure? Somewhere between 1 and 2 bars; 1.5 is ideal.

What if it's lower than that? You might have just bled your radiators, otherwise you could have a leak. Try rebalancing it following the steps in the manual.

If it's too high, will it blow up? Short answer – no. If it goes over 2.75 it should trigger the pressure-relief valve. Bleeding your radiators can also help.

Change a washer

I've fixed a few dripping taps with some success; often the problem is simply the rubber seal, which is easy to change. And it's good to be able to sort it out without having to pay call-out fees for something that takes minutes.

When it comes to screwing, unscrewing, loosening, or tightening, there is one golden rule that means you will always know which way to turn the screw/valve/bolt and so on. All you need to remember is:

Lefty loosey, righty tighty

Left to loosen or open things up. Right to tighten or close them. Simple!

I've honed my technique with stiff nuts, bolts, and screws thanks to my children: no one in my house can sit on a chair properly so the legs are always coming loose. I've had *lots* of practice fixing them. I'm now a dab hand with an Allen key and a pair of pliers.

That said, if it's a bigger problem or you genuinely don't know what you're doing, call in an expert to sort it or it could end up costing you more.

Note: *some taps use a ceramic cartridge rather than a washer. If this is the case, you'll need to buy a replacement cartridge from the supplier.*

TO CHANGE THE WASHER:

1   Turn off the water supply. If you forget to do this you'll be faced with a situation where water spurts out uncontrollably – hilarious in a cartoon, but not so amusing when it's your kitchen or bathroom that's under water. If you're working on a hot water tap, turn off the boiler (and immersion heater, if you have one) too.

2   Turn the tap on to drain any water left in the pipes.

3   Put the plug in – that way if you drop a vital screw you won't have to watch it disappear down the plughole.

4   Unscrew the cover from the tap to expose the valve, which should then be removed with a spanner.

5   The washer sits under the valve, held in place by a nut or screw. Use a spanner or screwdriver to remove it then replace with one of the same size.

6   Replace the valve and then the cover.

 Tip: *If you're in a tight spot and don't have a new washer, you can sometimes manage a quick fix by turning the washer over. If one side has perished less than the other, you can use this in the short term. But get a new washer as soon as you can!*

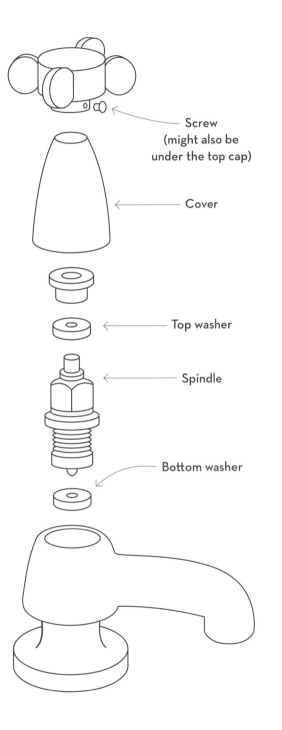

Screw
(might also be
under the top cap)

Cover

Top washer

Spindle

Bottom washer

HOW TO

Bleed a radiator

WHEN DO YOU NEED TO DO IT?
If your radiator is hot at the bottom but cold at the top it means trapped air is preventing it from working properly. Another sign might be sounds of rattling or gurgling.

WHAT EQUIPMENT DO YOU NEED?
- A mug or bucket
- An old towel or cloth
- A radiator key

Then what? If the heating's been on, wait for the radiator to cool down fully so you don't get burned by any water that you'll be draining out. Then:

1   Find the bleed valve (usually at the top on one end of the radiator - it looks a bit like a solid square sitting in a round hole). Set your mug or bucket beneath it and hold your cloth/towel directly below it to catch any drips.

2   Use the key to open the valve by turning it (slowly) anticlockwise. We have big, old, robust, school-style radiators where a quarter turn to the left is plenty (I've made that VERY clear).* It might hiss a bit as the air escapes. And drip a bit too. Trust me: even if you don't think it's working, DON'T open the valve too far (you will get wet) and don't even consider removing it altogether (you will get VERY wet).

3   When the hissing stops and water starts to come out, turn the key clockwise to close the valve.

*Lefty loosey coming into its own again!

Remember – don't fully remove the screw!

One Sunday morning when I was a teenager, my family and I were getting ready to go out. The big old-fashioned towel rail in the bathroom wasn't heating properly so I decided to be helpful and sort it out; I loved the idea of having a skill and knowing how to fix things. What could possibly go wrong?

Quite a lot, as it happened, starting with the fact that my 'skill' was theoretical rather than practical – and it turned out I wasn't as good at fixing things as I thought. My dad had shown me the basics, but what he hadn't done was hammer home the point that you are not supposed to remove the screw altogether. So I pulled it out; I thought it was bleeding very slowly, I was in a hurry, and I thought maybe if I could get it done faster everyone would be happy so taking it out would be the answer.

It was definitely not the answer.

The water was boiling hot, never-ending, just pouring out. I kept grabbing more and more towels to try to stem the flow but still it kept coming. It became clear the only way to stop it was to somehow get the screw back in. And I was going to have to do it myself; my parents, who had been waiting in the car and so were – at this stage – oblivious to what I was doing, had now given up and gone without me, so I just had to take a deep breath and go for it.

It was horrific. It wasn't clean water coming out, but a nasty brown ooze. It was all up the wallpaper – those were the days of wallpapered bathrooms – and the carpet was ruined (yes, we also had carpet in the bathroom). I burned myself too. So having learned my lesson at a cost, there was no way my girls were going to get away without knowing *exactly* how to bleed a radiator safely and without destroying the house in the process.

Deal with frozen pipes

There's a cold snap. Your pipes freeze. Suddenly this means there's no water supply to your home (not ideal if you want to shower, have a drink or flush the loo ...), but there could be worse to come. Sudden thaws can then cause the pipes to crack or burst. So frozen pipes are definitely something that it's good to avoid.

TO STOP YOUR PIPES FREEZING IN THE FIRST PLACE

1   Lag or insulate any pipes that are exposed to the cold. For instance, those located in unheated garages, lofts, or outside.

2   Keep your heating on at a low level (or on the frost-protection setting), including overnight, when the weather is particularly cold. If you are going away, don't turn the heating off completely, set the timer for it to come on for a burst each day and keep the thermostat set to 14°C.

IN COLD WEATHER WHEN THERE IS A DANGER THAT YOUR PIPES MIGHT FREEZE

1   Keep a bottle or container of drinking water in the fridge, just in case.

2   Know where your stopcock is, how to turn off the supply (see page 152) and make sure it works!

'Know where your stopcock is, how to turn off the supply, and make sure it works!'

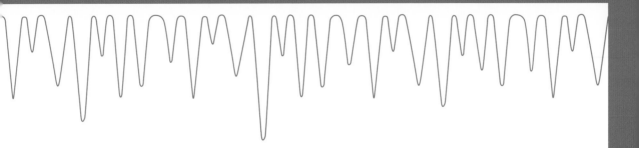

IF YOUR PIPES HAVE FROZEN

1   Turn off the water supply at the stopcock.

2   Turn on any cold taps nearby to help relieve the pressure on a pipe.

3   Thaw the pipe SLOWLY – starting at the end nearest the tap. This gives the water somewhere to go as it thaws.

4   Wrap a towel soaked in hot water around the frozen pipe, or place a hot water bottle on it. Never be tempted to pour boiling water over the pipe, as this could cause it to crack.

5   You can also use a hair dryer on its lowest setting, but don't use a blowtorch or anything else with a naked flame as again, this is likely to damage the pipes and could also cause a fire.

If the pipe is frozen somewhere that you don't have access to, try turning up the heat in the house and waiting. When the pipe has thawed, keep an eye on the area in the house where it is located for any signs of damp or water because of the pipe cracking.

IF A PIPE BURSTS

No matter how carefully you thaw a frozen pipe, it's not always possible to completely avoid damage. If you have a burst pipe, you should:

1   Turn off the mains water supply (see page 152). Whatever water is left in the pipes will still come out, but this will stop any more coming through.

2   If there is still a steady deluge it's likely the affected pipe is connected to your cold-water storage system. This means you need to drain the tank (these are usually found in loft spaces) before calling a plumber.

3   To drain the tank, turn on your cold taps until they run dry. You can also flush the toilet a number of times.

9

Electric dreams

I found Ava, aged 11, changing the light bulb in the bathroom

Now my girls just change them without prompting

Change a plug and a fuse

When the Covid-19 pandemic brought lockdown to the UK in 2020, I, like the rest of the country, got very into my internet shopping. Knowing I'd have to spend a lot more time at home, I bought two lamps to brighten things up a bit. It was only when they arrived that I discovered that they had the wrong kind of plugs. It was the perfect opportunity to show the girls how to change a plug – a really useful life skill that lots of adults don't seem to know, and one that's definitely worth brushing up on.

TO ATTACH A NEW PLUG

1   Remove the screws to take off the back of the plug and release the cable from the plug by loosening the screws on the cable grip (bit of plastic holding the cable in place).

2   Strip the end of the cable coming from the appliance into the plug, using wire strippers. You will need to strip about 3cm of the covering.

3   Separate the three wires inside from each other, and strip about 0.5–1cm off each using wire strippers, so that the copper wires are clearly visible.

4   Feed the flex through the cable grip of the new plug. You may need to loosen the cable grip with a screwdriver to fit the cable underneath – if so, tighten it again when you've connected the wires and the cable is ready to be secured in place.

5   Loosen the screws over the three wire holes, to give the wire space to connect with the metal contacts.

'Remember, if you are in the UK you should only use plugs that carry the BSI kitemark.'

6   Insert each wire into the correct hole.

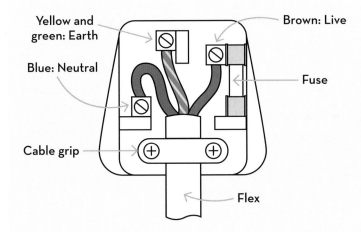

Yellow and green: Earth

Blue: Neutral

Brown: Live

Fuse

Cable grip

Flex

There's a simple trick to remember which wire goes where:

BLue = **B**ottom **L**eft

BRown = **B**ottom **R**ight

Striped goes in the middle.

7   Check that the cable grip has been tightened over the thick outer covering containing the three wires, rather than the exposed wires within. Then put the cover back on. Make sure the cover fits evenly and and is screwed tightly into place before using the appliance.

AND HERE'S THE LOWDOWN ON FUSES

A fuse can blow for a number of reasons: an electrical surge, faulty wiring or sockets. There may be too many appliances overloading the circuit at any one time (this happens to me constantly when I am doing the laundry). Or your appliance could be faulty, in which case the fuse will blow to cut the power and stop it overheating. To avoid problems with your fuses, you should make sure that the plug has the appropriate size fuse for the appliance (it can be dangerous to use the wrong one). The instructions should give you the necessary details, but as a rule of thumb:

• anything up to 700W (such as lamps or food mixers) takes a 3-amp fuse
• anything over 700W (such as an iron or a microwave) requires a 13-amp fuse.

If your fuse does blow and it needs changing, here's what to do:

1   Unscrew the cover of the plug using a screwdriver. Some plugs have a separate fuse cover – if this is the case, simply lever that off.

2   Lift out the old fuse and put the new one in its place, then replace the fuse or plug cover as appropriate. And that's it (unless it blows again, in which case you should get an electrician to take a look to find out why).

Change a light bulb

It's the subject of many a joke ... How many psychoanalysts does it take to change a light bulb? One, but the light bulb has to want to change. So while it's the stuff of urban myths, it's not always as easy as it looks, not least because there's a baffling array of bulbs out there (is there a degree course in light bulbs? There should be), and you first have to know which one you need.

They come in different shapes and sizes, with large bayonets and small bayonets, with thick screws and thin screws. And then there are spotlights, which can have different fittings again.

As if that wasn't enough, you need to know whether the bulbs you're fitting are:

- Halogen
- Energy saving (also known as CFL)
- LED

And then (possibly after a little lie down!) you also need to work out what wattage to go for depending on the type you've chosen. The labels can be confusing, but basically the equivalent of an old 60W bulb is 42W (halogen), 15W (energy saving), or 10W (LED).

But the first question to ask when changing your bulb is, is it an Edison (the screw or thread type) or a bayonet (known in our house as the prongy ones)? A screw bulb simply needs unscrewing - yes, there's a clue in the name - while to remove a bayonet you have to push it down (gently) and turn it anticlockwise to release it.

Tip – Take the old bulb with you when you go to buy a replacement – it saves you getting the wrong one and then having to go through the whole process again.

Edison or screw

!!! **DON'T FORGET:**
Check the labels on both the fixture and the bulb to make sure that the power rating of the bulb doesn't exceed that of the socket or fixture. (Also remember that some light shades should only be used with lower-wattage bulbs or they could catch fire. These are generally ones made from paper, canvas, or other flammable materials, but most shades will come with a sticker telling you what the maximum safe wattage of bulb is. Don't ignore this!)

When you have your bulb ready to go, there are a couple of safety precautions you need to take before you swap it.

Is the power off? For a ceiling light, turn the power off at the mains (you'll find the switch in your fuse box) to avoid any possibility of an electric shock. Lamps are much easier – just unplug them. When dealing with anything electrical, make sure you're wearing rubber soles and standing on wood!

Is the bulb hot? If it's only just gone, give it a couple of minutes to cool down. Burned hands don't help the process any. And they hurt. A lot.

How high? Lamps are obviously easy to get to; take out the old bulb, put in new bulb, done. But ceiling fixtures? Not always so simple. A stepladder is a good start, though it's important to have someone to hold it steady while you're up there. Don't be tempted to try to balance on something (a chair, a bed, or other piece of furniture), as it may well end in tears – or A&E.

To put in a screw bulb, simply screw it in a clockwise direction.

For a bayonet, align the two pins with the base, then push it in and gently twist upwards, in a clockwise direction. (As ever, with both types the lefty loosey, righty tighty rule comes into its own.)

Done!

Bayonet

Know your way round a fuse box

Our fuse box (now known as a 'consumer unit') trips whenever I have the washing machine, dryer, and iron on at the same time. A sign that I've overloaded the system, or that I should be doing something more exciting than laundry?

I'm usually upstairs when ours goes so it's in my interest that the girls – who are usually downstairs – know how to fix it. When teaching them I've made sure they've understood why it's happened in the first place, and what they can and (crucially) can't touch while they sort it out.

I've also taught them what to do if someone is electrocuted (see page 175).

The fuse box controls and distributes electricity around your home. It's also where you can switch the supply off (or on) in an emergency. Here's what you need to know:

1   Where it is! Sounds obvious, but if you've never had a problem, you might not have needed to know – until something goes wrong.

2   The most important switch is, helpfully, known as the mains switch. This is what turns the electricity supply off and on.

3   The key safety feature in your fuse box is the 'residual current device', or RCD, which monitors the currents in your home and will trip to turn off the circuit if it detects electricity flowing down an unintended path – such as a person who's touched a live wire. This protects against electric shock and can significantly reduce the risk of serious injury.

4   Circuit breakers (or fuses) work in a similar way by 'tripping', or automatically
    switching off. Each one controls a specific area of your home (such as downstairs
    lights, sockets in a specific area, and so on). You can see where the problem is at
    a glance, because one or more of the switches will be flicked down. To reset you
    simply flick them up again, though first you should identify the circuit (such as
    sockets in the kitchen) and unplug all the items on it.

5   After a couple of minutes, reset the switch and then plug in the items one at a
    time, switching them on to see whether they trip the circuit again. Once you've
    found the one causing the problem, try plugging it in on a different circuit. If it still
    doesn't work (or trips that circuit too), then the appliance is faulty and will need to
    be repaired or replaced. Note that some older fuse boxes have fuse wiring instead
    of circuit breakers. They work in much the same way by melting to break the circuit
    but the wire then needs to be replaced, which is something you should ask a trained
    electrician to do. It's not as easy as simply flicking a switch!

WHAT WORKS WHERE?

Different countries have different voltages. Some years ago the UK moved from
240v to 230v to be more in harmony with the rest of Europe (220v). This means
that you can use appliances such as hairdryers when travelling, as long as you have
an adapter plug where needed (sockets can vary in the number and shape of holes).
The USA and Canada supply voltage is 120v, so to use UK appliances in the US you
need a transformer or converter plug (these can be big and bulky). Don't use a US
hairdryer in the UK unless it's dual voltage – it's a sure way to blow a fuse (at best)
and can be downright dangerous.

HOW TO

Avoid getting electrocuted

When I was 15 I shorted the house by sticking a knife in the toaster. Luckily for me it had a plastic handle, otherwise I don't think I'd be here to tell the tale. It was such a stupid thing to do, so I've made sure to warn the kids about this and other actions with electrics that can be dangerous:

- **Never** stick knives or other metal objects in the toaster.

- **Never** plug in phones or other electrics near baths (or hairdryers near showers, etc). It's very easy to drag a cable through into the bathroom, but don't even think about it.

- **Never** use extension cords near a sink/bath/swimming pool/paddling pool.

- **Never** use electrical items/plug things in if you are wet from the bath or shower (or have wet hands).

- **Never** use an electrical appliance if the cord (or plug) is damaged.

- **Never** poke anything (especially something metal) into a plug socket.

- **Always** switch off the appliance and socket before unplugging something.

'Most electrical burns are to the hands and feet. Do not bandage, but apply clean, sterile gauze. If patient is showing signs of shock, such as fainting, elevate their legs. Keep the patient warm.'

If someone has been electrocuted

If you think someone has been electrocuted, do not touch them until the contact or circuit has been broken or you will get electrocuted too.

1   Turn off the electricity if possible.

2   If you can't turn it off, move the person away from the source of the shock by using something that won't conduct electricity, such as a wooden stick or broom handle.

3   If you still can't break contact, try looping fabric or rope around their arms or ankles to pull them to safety. Remember: do not touch them.

4   Get someone to call 999 and treat any injuries in the meantime (see pages 98–119).

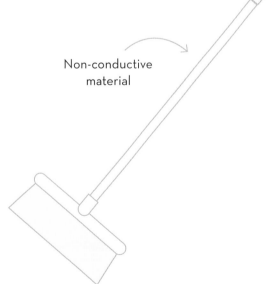

Non-conductive
material

10

Home front

Hero, aged 7, learning how to smelt iron. She came home with a very heavy paperweight

Hero, aged 5, painting her stepsister's room – a lovely surpr͏ and something she was proud to a͏

Hero, aged 8, building a table with my partner, Sim

Hero, aged 6, fixing the doorknob with the correct screwdriver

Hero, aged 6, assembling an ottoman, and using the headlamp from her survival kit

Get rid of moths

We recently lived through 'Mothgate', and it was not fun, although thankfully our moths had very cheap taste when it came to clothing. The kids got as obsessed as me about counting them and seeing how many we had captured every morning. But then we found them in the carpets and I thought, that's it now – we are overrun. There were holes in everything and the carpet started to get bald patches, so in the end I had to call in the professionals.

Spraying felt like we were doing something, though it wasn't completely successful. (There is a way to remove them once and for all; the professionals bring in specialist equipment but they turn the heat up in the house so high that any plastics, lipsticks, and toiletries in the room will melt – which put us off a bit.) So now all of us are on constant moth watch and using pretty much every preventative option on the market.

KNOW YOUR ENEMY
It's not actually the moths that snack on your clothes and carpets, but their larvae. They're only about a millimetre long when they hatch, so they're easy to miss ... until the holes start to appear. So how do you stop them before they eat their way through your wardrobe?

1   **HERBAL REMEDIES**
    Lavender, rosemary, and thyme act as a natural deterrent to moths. They smell good (unless you're a moth), so they offer a fragrant alternative to the stinky mothballs of old. I use the sachets and the balls. You can keep dried leaves and flower buds in a small cloth bag, hung in your wardrobe, or use an essential oil diffuser.

2   **CEDAR**
    Also smells good (again, unless you're a moth, in which case you'll be repelled by the pheromones and won't lay your eggs anywhere nearby). You can get cedar furniture or chests, but there are smaller-scale options, too, such as cedar rings to put round hooks on hangers, and blocks or balls to keep in cupboards and drawers. It's the oil that repels moths, so keep the wood well sanded and replenish the oil every three months or so to keep them at bay.

3 CLEANING

Moths love dust or dirt, so a thorough clean and vacuum will make your carpets much less hospitable. Just make sure you wash any cloths and dusters that you use well, and empty the vacuum bag to get rid of any eggs or larvae you've picked up.

4 FREEZING

Larvae love fabric but apparently not fish fingers – so stick any clothes showing tell-tale signs in the freezer for at least 24 hours. The cold will see them off.

5 HEAT

A 60°C (+) wash and the highest setting on the dryer should polish off even the hardiest larvae. Although only use this technique on clothes that won't shrink at those temperatures. There's not much point in getting rid of the critters only to find your favourite top will now only fit a 2-year-old. I speak from experience.

6 VINEGAR

Use white rather than malt – both for efficacy and because you don't want your bedroom to smell like a chippy. Mix a 1:1 solution with water and scrub the insides of your wardrobes and drawers with it.

7 PRODUCTS

You can buy special pads and hangers to combat moths. These, conversely, use pheromones to attract and trap male moths and stop them from reproducing. We tried loads of plug-ins with a little light. They are great, although you do feel like you're living in a kebab shop. Ultrasonic plug-ins send out waves to keep moths away (but can't be heard by human ears).

8 PRAY TO THE MOTH GODS

The kids and I resorted to this at the height of our infestation, though it's not terribly effective on its own. But every little helps and all that.

Get rid of cooking fat

Headlines and news footage like in 2019 about the 40-tonne 'fatberg', the size of a double-decker bus, being dug out of a London sewer should have been enough to put anyone off roasting or frying for life. But then ... chips. Roast potatoes ... Crispy exteriors and hot fluffy centres ... Filipino turon (bananas wrapped in spring-roll pastry and fried) ... Could there be a better incentive to find more environmentally friendly ways to get rid of cooking fat and oil than simply pouring them down the sink?

LUCKILY, THERE ARE SOME SIMPLE SOLUTIONS

1   Try to reuse your oil until it's had it before getting rid of it to minimize the number of times you need to do dispose of it, and the amount you dispose of. Strain the used oil into a container through a sieve to remove any bits from cooking, then use as needed. It's a money-saving tip, but it also helps to prevent creating fatbergs of the future.

2   Turn it into bird food! Lard and suet are both great for this. You'll need birdseed and some fat at room temperature, then combine these at a ratio of about one part fat to two parts seed before cooling and shaping into cakes or balls. The RSPB has lots of great recipes that include other household staples such as porridge oats.

3   Wait for fats like butter, lard, and dripping to solidify and then add these to your food recycling.

4   Check whether your local council has a scheme to collect used oil. If they do, keep it in an old, wide-necked container until you have enough to take to your local disposal or recycling service.

5   If only a small quantity of oil has been used, mop it up with some paper towels (ideally recycled ones) to absorb it all, then put in the bin. For larger amounts you can pour the used fat into a container then seal it before throwing it in the bin (old cooking oil bottles and similar are good for this). Unless you are using a container that can't be recycled anyway, this is not terribly environmentally friendly, but it is a good way to avoid blocking your pipes. If you're using a plastic bottle or tub, make sure the fat is cool first – melting the container as you pour will only throw up a whole new set of issues.

Wash up

In our house – and probably yours too – you can always tell who's done the washing up by how much residue is left on the dishes! We have a dishwasher – I've now taught the baby to unload the plates. Result! – but when it comes to pots and pans, Sim and I have very different approaches. I like to get in there and wash everything immediately, whereas he likes to make dish soup and just leave it to soak. You can see the film building up.

I'm a bit paranoid about it all after seeing a video recently where someone took a 'clean' wooden spoon and put it in a glass of boiling water. The stuff that came off it was disgusting! This is why metal utensils are always good!

So, this is the technique that I find works best for getting things squeaky clean:

1 Scrape as much off the dishes/pans as you can before putting them into the hot soapy water.

2 Always do glasses first, followed by plates, and leave the most heavily soiled items until last.

3 If pans, roasting tins, and so on are ingrained with stuck-on food, fill them with hot soapy water and let them soak while you do everything else. This will make it much easier to remove the stubborn bits.

4 Rinse your washed items in clean hot water, making sure you get all the suds off.

5 Dry (or, if you are me, leave to drip dry on the side ... I always feel like I'm in a movie or a sitcom when I start drying the dishes!).

MY FAVOURITE TIPS

- **Bicarbonate of soda** is brilliant on tins after doing a Sunday roast, but I've started using it on pots and pans, too. Sprinkle it on any stubborn, cooked-on bits of food, and leave it to soak.

- **Vinegar**. I've got a spritzer now filled with white vinegar. It's great for shifting stubborn stains. I love it so much I've started buying massive two-litre bottles of the stuff.

Know your way around a toolbox

It's no secret that I love my toolbox. Over the years I've had my fair share of mishaps and injuries, but the one thing they've taught me is that you should never use the wrong tool for the job. If you have a properly stocked toolbox you will never have to improvise!

THESE ARE MY MUST-HAVES

Screwdrivers – I use them all the time, whether it's for hanging picture frames, fixing the doorknobs that the kids hang everything off, attaching hooks, taking toys apart and putting them back together. My daughter Hero is phenomenal. If one of my son's toys needs new batteries she gets very excited about having to go and get the screwdriver, use lefty loosey, righty tighty (see page 158) to open it up, figure out what battery she needs and get it working again. **DO** get both flat head (which lives up to its name and has ... a flat head) and Phillips screwdrivers. **DON'T** think you can cut corners by using a knife instead. One slip and that's it – disaster. Apart from the fact that you run the risk of losing a finger:

a) cutlery wasn't designed to undo screws and so it's basically rubbish at it; and
b) if you keep jabbing at the screw with the wrong tool you'll end up bending or breaking it, which can make it almost impossible to remove (at least until you use a power tool to drill it out, which then ends up ruining whatever it was sitting in in the first place).

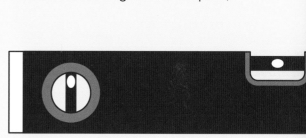

A 5m tape measure – this basically does what it says on the tin and is another thing that I use all the time. Useful for measuring many things, including spaces if you're planning to buy furniture. If it's something large, it's even more useful for measuring the entrance to the room. It's soul-destroying to wait six weeks for your dream sofa only to find you can't actually get it through the door.

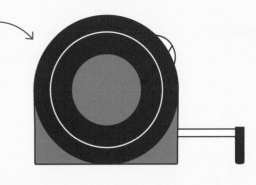

For more measuring fun, try seeing how far your hands can stretch on a piano. Standard reach is 8 notes (an octave) or 9, though Rachmaninov could manage 13 – the length of a piece of A4 paper or a kitchen spoon (around 297mm if you were wondering).

A claw hammer – another essential when it comes to putting up pictures, mirrors, and so on. If your attempts to hang a mirror always seem to go awry, you'll find the other end (the 'claw') is perfect for removing all the nails that are in the wrong place.

Spanners and/or a wrench – good for household stuff – loosening and tightening taps, nuts, and bolts. The main thing to remember is pull rather than push. The skin on your knuckles will thank you.

A spirit level – to show whether the picture/mirror/shelf you spent the last hour putting up is level. If it is, the little bubble will fall between the two marked lines in the centre. If it isn't, the claw bit of the hammer (and the tape measure) will come in handy to help fix it.

Continued overleaf →

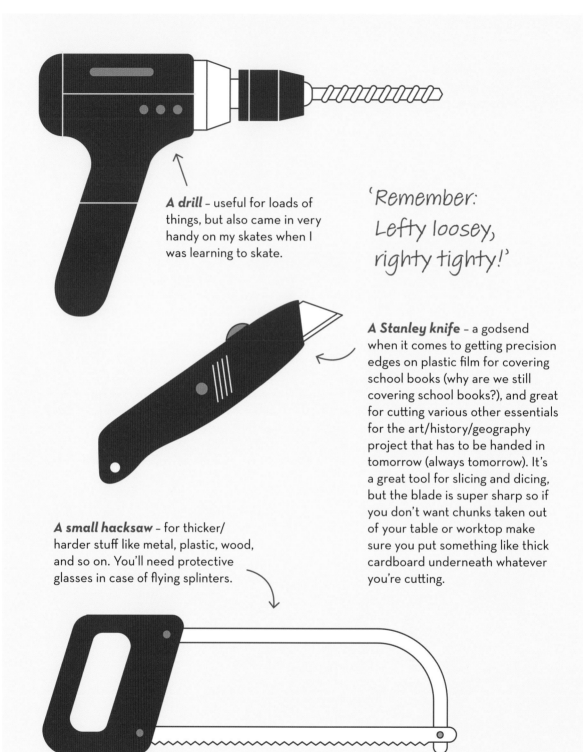

A drill – useful for loads of things, but also came in very handy on my skates when I was learning to skate.

'Remember: Lefty loosey, righty tighty!'

A Stanley knife – a godsend when it comes to getting precision edges on plastic film for covering school books (why are we still covering school books?), and great for cutting various other essentials for the art/history/geography project that has to be handed in tomorrow (always tomorrow). It's a great tool for slicing and dicing, but the blade is super sharp so if you don't want chunks taken out of your table or worktop make sure you put something like thick cardboard underneath whatever you're cutting.

A small hacksaw – for thicker/harder stuff like metal, plastic, wood, and so on. You'll need protective glasses in case of flying splinters.

Know your batteries

I always have a selection of spare batteries in the house, whether they're for TV remotes, toys, or doorbells (as I write, I just fixed mine – Phillips screwdriver, lithium battery, and connected it up to the Wi-Fi. Job done). In fact, in my family I'm famous for my special drawer of essentials (it's a joy!) that everyone laughs at but also digs into whenever they need a battery or a light bulb.

There are two main types of battery:

1   **Alkaline batteries.** These are the most common type (accounting for 80% of battery sales in the UK) and the standard sizes are AA, AAA – which are the two we use the most – but also C, D, and 9V.

2   **Lithium.** Lithium coin batteries are used in things like car keys, bathroom scales, remote-controlled toys, and so on. They are generally labelled with the letters CR followed by four numbers. The first two denote the diameter in millimetres and the second two the thickness. For example, a CR2025 battery is 20mm diameter and 2.5mm thick. It's essential to keep these batteries well away from babies and pets – they're super dangerous and if swallowed can cause corrosive burns that can be fatal. I keep mine safely locked away from little fingers.

I've talked about why lithium batteries need to be kept away from young children, and my girls loved learning about it. There was a campaign recently where they put a lithium battery between two pieces of ham to demonstrate what happens if you swallow one. My innate fear, and my kids' caution, has been hugely exacerbated by that so we are all, always, super careful.

Hang a picture

This is something that it took me a long time to figure out – although after you have learned how to do it properly you do wonder why you made such a song and dance about it for years on end. I hang up all my girls' music certificates, and when they are all lined up there together it's obviously important to know how to get them exactly where you want them rather than ending up with an undulating row that just looks a mess. I have now taught them to hang their own, too. They find it really motivating to see what they've achieved – and really satisfying to be able to add another one to the row.

This is how to get your pictures hanging where you actually want them:

1   Decide exactly where you want the top of the frame to sit.

2   Make a small, light pencil mark around the two top corners. This will be easy to rub out afterwards as long as you use a clean rubber, otherwise your paintwork won't thank you.

3   Hold the cord or wire on the back of the picture in the middle and pull the centre up so it's taut – you don't need to add much tension but then you will see how far it will go when it sits on the nail.

4   Measure that point to the top of the frame – and that's the distance your nail needs to go below where you want the top of the frame to sit.

In the past, before I mastered this, I tried all sorts of ridiculously complicated measurements and calculations. I've drawn round the frame, I've used spirit levels – the lot. I started putting pictures up when I was about 15 and didn't really get the gist of it until I moved into my second flat when I was about 22 – yep, it took me that long and all the time it really was that simple!

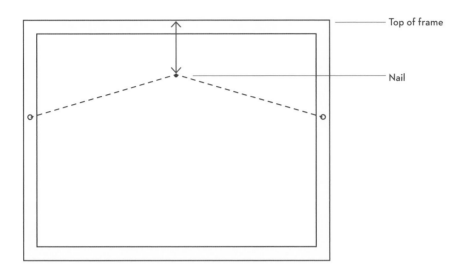

Top of frame

Nail

RAWL PLUGS

I love a rawl plug! Put them in a drilled hole and they spring out to grip the inside of the wall ... they're ingenious! If you're hanging something heavy or fixing it onto a crumbly surface such as brick or plasterboard, where the screw might be rattling round in the wall without enough traction to hold, then they're essential to make sure the fittings stay firm. You should always use them for things like mirrors and shelves.

You need to make sure that:

1   The rawl plug is the right size for the screws you are using. Lighter things like picture frames will require smaller screws than, say, a shelf or cabinet. Screws have a 'gauge' – such as 4, 8, 10 – with metric equivalents in millimetres, though they don't correspond with the gauge numbers, which can be confusing! Plugs come in various colours, but as a general rule, yellow plugs take smaller screws (3–4mm), red, medium (4–5mm), and brown, larger (up to 6mm). But this can vary, so always check the label carefully.

2   The plug fits the hole you've drilled tightly, but it doesn't need more than a little pressure from your finger to push it most of the way in.

3   The top of the plug is flush with the wall before you put the screw in – you may need to tap it (gently!) with a hammer to achieve this.

Continued overleaf →

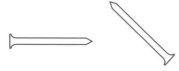

WIRES AND PIPES

The first rule of banging anything into the wall is to check that you're not going to hit a cable or a pipe. It's not always easy to know where these are – you should be particularly careful with walls that connect to kitchens or bathrooms.

You can buy electric wire detectors, which will help you avoid areas that contain cables. But if you don't have one, a good rule of thumb is:

1   Turn the electricity off before you start hammering/drilling.

2   Avoid sticking nails directly above light switches and plug sockets, or anywhere in the vertical line above them where the cables might lie.

When my girls are putting things up I also make sure that they hold on to the rubber bit of the hammer, just in case. If you're touching the metal part and accidentally hit a wire you could easily electrocute yourself.

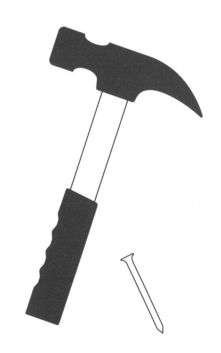

Tip: You can also buy stud finders to help you find something solid to put your nail into when hanging something heavy, rather than just thin plasterboard. They will save you making lots of unnecessary holes in your wall while looking for said studs.

Fill holes in walls

——

Anyone who has yet to learn the art of picture hanging must also be well-versed in the art of filling in the holes that all the ill-fated nails leave behind, or those of previous residents of your home. Suffice to say, before I got good at hanging pictures, I got very good at *this* very quickly.

(This method is also good for filling small cracks. For big ones, replastering might be necessary, but only after you've checked what's caused the crack in the first place.)

The first rule when you've put a nail in the wrong place is to pull it out with pliers or the claw part of your hammer. NEVER wiggle it to get it out (either with pliers/claw hammer or fingers!), as you will make the hole much worse.

To fix small holes in plaster or plasterboard walls, all you need to do is:

1   Use a little bit of filler to plug the gap.

2   Once the filler is dry, smooth away any rough edges with a bit of sandpaper, dust it off, and then you are ready to paint over it.

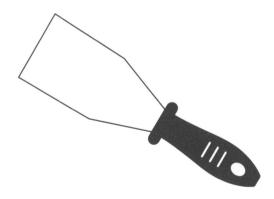

Know your paint types

With my dad away a lot with his job, a lot of little maintenance jobs didn't always get done around the house – unless I did them!

My introduction to decorating came at 14. Our wallpaper had seen better days and was hanging off the wall, and when my friends came over and saw it, they laughed. I was completely mortified and determined to do something about it.

So I went out to buy paint. The man in the shop was my guru – he really took me under his wing, and I got my DIY education right there and then. My talent for decorating was born from humiliation and necessity, but I did it, and once I'd stripped away the wallpaper and painted the wall, it looked brilliant. So, here's a quick guide to paint, and what you need for whichever bit of wall or woodwork you're painting:

UNDERCOAT
This provides a light, even surface for your paint to go onto, and makes the finished wall look a lot better – especially if you're painting over a dark colour or a surface that's marked or stained.

EMULSION
Generally used on walls and ceilings. It's easier to remove fingerprints and pen marks from the ones that offer a washable finish, though satin/silk finishes (which have a bit more of a sheen) can also be harder-wearing than basic matt.

EGGSHELL
For woodwork such as doors and window frames. Not as shiny as gloss.

GLOSS
For woodwork again – and it's shiny. *(A cautionary tale – if you are renting and use magnolia gloss to try to patch up the bits where Sellotape has taken the paint off a wall painted in magnolia emulsion, don't expect to get your deposit back.)*

GOLDEN RULES I LEARNED FROM THE MAN IN THE SHOP

- You will need two or three coats to get an even finish.

- Although you can wash brushes used with water-based paints under the tap, if you've used oil-based paints you'll need white spirit (in which case make sure you read the label on the bottle and handle with care). Always dry brushes thoroughly before reusing them or putting them away.

- Store brushes vertically (handle down, bristles up), or hang them so the bristles don't get damaged.

Now I've taught the girls everything I know – they're experts at cutting in and (just as importantly) cleaning up after themselves.

Cutting in is when you use a brush to cover areas that are too tight to be done with a roller, such as along the skirting and ceiling lines, corners, and any narrow areas – for example around door frames.

You're midway through painting, but you want to make a cuppa/eat dinner/ make a phone call? Keep your brushes from drying out by wrapping them tightly in cling film or popping them into a sealable plastic bag.

11

Motorways

Getting a friend's car out of the mud while keeping my dress clean

Clearing a roadblock in the Himalayas with Save the Children, before helping to change a tyre on the mountainside

Hero, aged 5, helping me to check the car

Teaching the girls how to check the tyres, under supervision of course. Hero, aged 8 and Ava, aged 12

On the road with an NGO in the Democratic Republic of Congo

Stuck in the mud in the Democratic Republic of Congo – another tyre change

Jump-start a car

Getting a flat battery is frustrating enough. Having to find someone to sort it out for you is even more so. If you have the knowledge and the jump leads, all you need is someone with a working engine and you can get it sorted way quicker than having to hang on for a patrol van.

I don't want my girls ever having to stand on a hard shoulder for two hours on their own waiting for someone to help them, so it's important for me that they know the theory behind how it works. Jump leads and car batteries are absolutely things that shouldn't be messed with, so their hands-on experience can wait until they are of an age to drive. But when our neighbour had a flat battery in lockdown it offered the perfect chance to give them a demonstration of what goes where, and for them to see the spark and not be frightened of it. (It can be unnerving – I know plenty of adults who feel the same way.)

WHAT YOU'LL NEED
The aforementioned jump leads. And someone with a car with a fully charged battery that they can (ideally) park bumper to bumper with yours.

USEFUL TO REMEMBER
The RED lead is the positive one and the BLACK one is negative.

WHAT TO DO

1   Make sure the key's been removed from the ignition, no one is smoking nearby, and the battery isn't damaged or leaking. If it is, you'll need to speak to a mechanic/recovery service.

2   Attach the red lead to the positive (+) battery terminal on the charged battery in the other car, then attach the other end to the same point in yours.

'Never remove the jump leads while the car engine is running.'

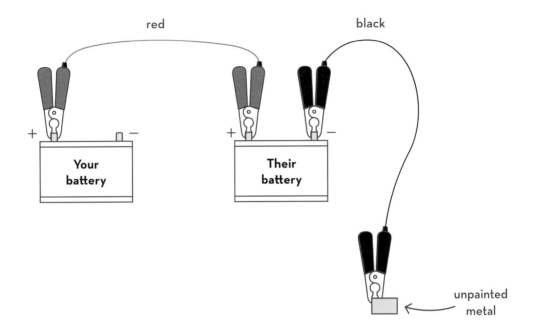

red   black

Your battery

Their battery

+   −   +   −

unpainted metal

3   Connect the black cable to the negative (-) terminal on the working car, but this time DON'T attach the other end to your car. Instead, put the clamp onto a solid piece of metal away from the battery/fuel system. Some cars have an 'earthing rod' specifically for this purpose. If yours does, your manual will show you where it is.

4   When you've done that, wait for 5 minutes before starting the working engine. Let it run for a minute then try starting your car. If nothing happens, give it another couple of minutes and try again.

5   When your engine starts, leave both cars running for 10 minutes or so (it goes without saying not to leave them unattended). Then you can remove the clamps in reverse order: black lead from your car, black lead from the other car; red lead from your car, red lead from the other car. Be very careful not to touch any metal components as you do this.

6   Let your engine run for another 15–20 minutes so that it doesn't lose power again, then take it for a 30-minute drive.

Get a car out of the mud

I was at a wedding when a friend's car got stuck in the mud. Cue general panic and despair. But I was very proud to be the one to get it out (without getting covered in mud myself – a definite bonus). I rolled my dress up, tucked it into the sides of my knickers, put on my trainers, found a tow rope in the church hall – and hey presto. I lost my rubber floor mats in the process, but got a huge cheer when I arrived victorious at the reception.

So here's what to do (if you can beg the help of a car that's not stuck!):

1   Make sure all passengers are out of the car. You want to reduce the weight of the car as much as possible – plus, you need them to help push and pull!

2   Attach the front of your car to the back of a car that isn't stuck using a sturdy length of rope.

3   Grab the floor mats from inside your car (the ones from the front are generally bigger, so are better to use here), then put them as far under your wheels as you can. You can use cardboard, too, but not everyone has large pieces of this handily tucked away in their boot, and most cars have mats.

4   Make sure the stuck car has the handbrake off! The front car should now drive off slowly, taking up the slack on the rope and then pulling the other one out. The crucial thing here is for the driver of the front car NOT to slam the brakes on when they meet resistance – that ruins the process as you need the momentum to pull out the stranded car. It's tempting to pause, but you just have to keep going, slowly and steadily – and it works!

'Do not be so pleased with yourself that you then drive off and forget to get your mats back. Mine were sadly lost to the muddy field.'

If there are no other cars around to help:

1   Try to create some space for your tyres by moving the steering wheel back and forth before you press down on the accelerator to move the car forward.

2   Don't be tempted to put your foot down and rev the engine, as this will only cause the wheels to spin and make matters worse.

3   Use the mats as above if needed.

4   When you do get free, drive away slowly in second gear. Wait until the excess mud has come off your tyres before increasing your speed.

Check the pressure on car tyres

This is a really useful skill to have in your arsenal. I like teaching my kids plenty of things, but this isn't something they should be doing on their own. However, it's still good for them to understand what you're doing, so if you find yourself needing to check your tyres and put air in them, it's a great thing to talk through when you're doing it.

WHY DOES PRESSURE MATTER?

Essentially, it keeps you safe. If your tyres aren't pumped up properly it can affect their grip and the way you handle the car, potentially leading to accidents, as well as blow outs. It's also worth knowing that tyres wear out more quickly if they're not at the correct pressure – and your fuel costs are likely to be higher because the car needs more force to turn. Overinflation can cause problems with wheel alignment and greater wear on the tyres, which can put you at risk of losing control when you drive at high speeds.

HOW DO YOU KNOW WHAT THE CORRECT PRESSURE IS?

It varies between car models, depending on the size, weight, and so forth, so it's really important to know what's right for your own vehicle before you get started. You should be able to find the details somewhere on your car. Mine is stamped on the sill of the driver's door down near the tyres. Some cars have it printed inside the fuel tank flap. It can also be found in your vehicle handbook and, if all else fails, there are websites where you can enter your registration details and it will come up with the figures you need. It's usually shown as **PSI** – which stands for pounds per square inch.

HOW DO YOU CHECK THE PRESSURE?

Most garages have a tyre-pressure gauge and it's always worth checking all four tyres on a regular basis. To do this:

1   Remove the valve cap and put it somewhere safe. It's small and easy to lose!

2   Attach the gauge to the valve and enter the number that the tyre should be set at.

3   If you need more air, add it before replacing the cap.

4   If the pressure is too high, let out some air until it hits the correct amount. The gauge should sound to let you know when it's correct.

5   Replace the cap.

'If your tyres aren't pumped up properly it can affect their grip and the way you handle the car.'

CHECK YOUR TYRE PRESSURE!

My friend took my girls and her own daughter to the zoo and called me as she'd had a blow out on the motorway on the way there. I was at work and remember being terrified for them all. She had managed to steer the car onto the hard shoulder and call for help. My girls literally only remember one thing about it all; they were allowed to dig into the food bag for ham sandwiches which they ate on the grassy bank while waiting for the rescue services. But blow outs are scary and can be dangerous.
Check your PSI!

Change the tyre on a car

Most of my car shenanigans I've learned (the hard way) on trips with Save the Children. On one occasion we were high in the Himalayas when we had to drive past another vehicle on a treacherously narrow bit of road. The solution? The driver took two planks of wood out of the boot, placed them in front of the car – suspended over the abyss – and drove over them. It was the only way you could overtake. My heart was in my mouth. I was convinced we weren't going to make it. It was the scariest experience of my life, and then, after a mini heart attack, I discovered that these things tend to come in threes: not long afterwards we found the road barricaded by a fallen tree and had to get out and remove that; the final hurdle was a puncture.

The tyres were huge and heavy so it was a two-person job – and those two people were me and the driver. One of the wheel nuts was really tight so I jumped up and down on the wrench/wheel brace, which everyone found hilarious. All the locals gathered round to watch the show, so I really wanted to get it right!

Luckily I had learned a lot as a child when my dad seemed to spend half his time under the car with just his legs poking out. Every now and then an arm would reach out for various different kinds of tools and I had to make sure I passed him the correct one. It all comes down to knowing your tools.

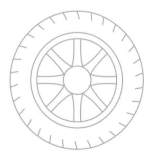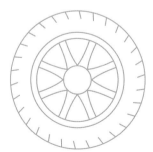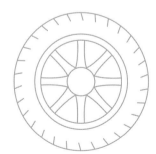

So if you get a puncture and you need to change the entire wheel, these are the steps to follow:

1   Switch off the engine, put your handbrake on, and get all your passengers out. Then put the car into reverse.

2   Find the spare wheel and your tools. Usually the spare wheel is in the boot, and the appropriate tools should be with it, but this is a good reminder to check before you need them in an emergency! Put a chock (a special wedge to stop a wheel from moving) under the wheel that's diagonally opposite the one you're changing, to stop the wheel rolling when you jack up the car. If you don't have a chock, you can use rocks or bricks instead.

3   Loosen the wheel nuts – this is the bit that needs the strength, as well as the locking wheel-nut key.

'Remember: lefty loosey!'

4   Position your jack on the same side of the car as the wheel you're replacing. If you can put something solid like a plank of wood under the jack to keep it stable, even better.

5   Jack the car up slowly until it's about 10cm off the ground.

6   Remove the wheel nuts and then take off the wheel by pulling it towards you.

7   Put the new wheel on, replace the wheel nuts, and tighten by hand.

'That's righty tighty!'

8   Gently lower the car using the jack so the new tyre just touches the ground, and then finish tightening the wheel nuts with your wrench/wheel brace.

9   Finish lowering, remove the jack, and you're done. Just remember to put your tools away and remove the chock before you drive off. And remember to return the spare wheel to the boot when you have the new tyre replaced at a garage, so you still have a spare.

12

Food for thought

The locals on the Yap Islands kindly prepared a feast in honour of our crew

Check it's cooked in the middle. Nothing to smile about

Ava and Hero, aged 8 and 5, always baking

Ava, aged 5, joining in the celebrations — drinking water at my BFF's wedding

Perfectly cooked pasta. Ava and Hero, aged 7 and 4

A milkshake with all the trimmings. Not going to think about the sugar content

Knives, forks, fingers

Typically on holidays, cocktails are stronger and alcohol content can be disguised

Never imagined I'd have dinner with Prince Charles, after performing for him, but it actually happened

Practising spaghetti-twirling. Hero, aged 7

Read a food label

Expiry dates are my bible. I will cremate anything even close to its use-by date just to be safe. 'Overcook rather than undercook' is my motto! And if it goes a minute over the date, that's it. I won't touch it with a barge pole (although Sim is much more gung-ho. On the plus side, this does mean no food waste).

But other than that, I try not to be governed by labels too much. We know that broccoli is good for you and trifle is not quite so good for you without reading the details. It is worth noting, though, that labels can sometimes be deceptive at first glance if you're not sure what you're looking at. Who hasn't tucked into a large bag of chocolates showing a surprisingly low-calorie value on the front, only to then read it properly and discover that this isn't for the whole bag or even half of it, but for just one portion that turns out to be three measly pieces?

Most packaged food comes with two labels: the one on the back is all about ingredients and should have a full list, with allergens marked in bold. That can obviously be hugely useful. The one on the front is all about the nutrition: how healthy the food is, how much fat, salt, or sugar it might contain, and how that relates to our recommended daily intakes.

This will include:

CALORIES
Energy values are generally shown in kJ (kilojoules) and kcal (kilocalories), although most of us are more familiar with the latter (aka calories). Recommended daily intakes are 2,000 for a woman and 2,500 for a man, whereas for children there's a range according to age and gender – for instance, a 7-year-old girl/boy would need 1,510–1,649, while a 10-year-old girl/boy would need 1,936–2,032.

FAT
This is usually divided into saturated fat (the bad kind that clogs your arteries) and unsaturated (the good kind that helps lower cholesterol, build strong cell membranes and more). A food is high in fat if it contains more than 17.5g of fat per 100g, and low in fat if it contains 3g or under.

CARBOHYDRATES

These often show sugars (less good) and fibre (important) separately. As with fat, protein, and salt, the figures shown are usually per 100g, though often labels also show calories and nutrients per portion, too. A high sugar content is more than 22.5g per 100g.

SALT

Adults should eat no more than a teaspoon (or 6g salt, which contains 2.4g of sodium) a day. This is harder to stick to you than you'd think, as it's added to practically every processed food. For children, the recommended limit is 2–3g salt depending on age. Babies under one should avoid salt altogether. High salt (which can play havoc with blood pressure, putting you at risk of heart disease and stroke) is more than 1.5g per 100g (or 0.6g of sodium).

Essentially, it's good to eat foods that are low in salt, sugar, and hydrogenated fat and best to limit those that have high levels of these things. But with all this in mind, I think the most important thing of all is to develop a healthy relationship with food in the first place.

A HAPPY, HEALTHY KITCHEN

I want my children to enjoy eating. I want them to keep fit and be strong mentally and physically. Food is the fuel for that; you can't run, think properly, or manage your mood without the right fuel. A balanced diet is essential to achieve this, though I don't believe in forbidden foods. We don't make diet a big thing or talk about 'naughty' foods or eating less to fit into an item of clothing. Cake and biscuits taste good (so good). Sure, they're not great for nutrients, but they're great in moderation. It's all about getting the mix right.

Times are very different from when I was growing up and another thing I never do is make my children finish everything on their plates. How do I know how hungry they were to start with or how full they might be feeling? It's all about balance. I might say if you want pudding (Hero always wants pudding), you need to have one more mouthful, but I never beat them with a head of broccoli to make them clear the whole lot.

And it's important to remember that we are all different shapes and sizes, so there's no point comparing. I know mothers who compare their figures to their daughters'. It's ludicrous. I'm in my forties and have had three kids! You can forget that. Also, I really like trifle. Throw out your bathroom scales. I don't discuss diets or ever weigh myself. Kids learn from watching you and how you see yourself in the mirror. Try to see the best of yourself so they can learn to do the same.

Set a table

It sounds so simple, but in actual fact setting a table is a really important life skill. People can be intimidated by more formal place settings, but once you know what goes where you never have to worry when you are seated in front of an array of cutlery at a posh dinner.

I have a friend who uses my bread plate every single time – now whenever we have dinner I have to race for it before he can get to it. Why don't I say anything? Having told the kids that it's bad manners to point out other people's bad manners, I feel I have to stick to it.

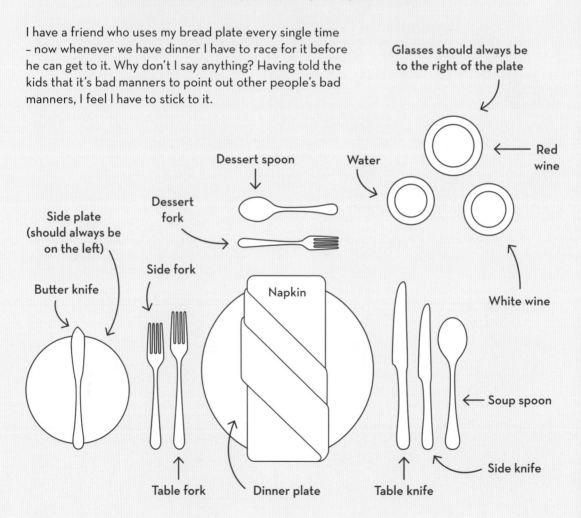

Knowing about table settings can be seen as snobbery, but it's a good thing to learn and you never know when it might come in handy. I had dinner with Prince Charles after playing the harp for him – not something I ever thought I would do, but I was very glad I knew what was what when I was sat at the table.

There's an etiquette around how to use the various utensils, too. Here are some dos and don'ts:

- Never use your fork as a shovel – the tines (or prongs) should always face down and not up, unless you're actually putting something in your mouth; instead use your knife to push things like peas onto the top of it.

- On which note – if things (like peas) are tricky to keep on the fork, try squashing them first, coating them in a sauce to help them 'stick' or mashing them into softer foods such as potato.

- Never put your knife in your mouth. If you're tempted to lick something off it, simply scrape whatever it is onto your fork instead.

- It's fine to eat pasta using just a fork.

- If you have a spoon and fork for your dessert, use the spoon to break it up into bite-size pieces and the fork to push the bits onto your spoon if needed. If it's something soft, such as ice cream or mousse, just a spoon is absolutely fine.

Tip: *I have taught my girls a few handy extras, too. Do you know why wine glasses have stems? It's so we can hold them securely without touching the bulb – as that would affect the temperature of the wine. There are different glasses for red and white wine, because red needs a wider bulb to help the wine breathe. And I've also made sure they know that a napkin goes on their lap and is not waved around like a flag or tucked into the neck of their top, both of which would be frowned upon at a formal dinner.*

'Having told the kids that it's bad manners to point out other people's bad manners, I feel I have to stick to it.'

Carve a chicken/turkey

My dad's work often took him away over Christmas, and so the job of carving the turkey came to me. It was hard for us that he wasn't around at that special time of year, so I tried to take the role seriously and deliver perfect slices rather than hacking the bird to bits. It's served me well over the years – perfect slices every time.

1   Before you start, allow the chicken or turkey to rest for at least 15 minutes after taking it out of the oven. You can cover it in foil to keep it warm. This allows the juices to settle and keeps the meat moist and easy to cut.

2   Make sure the bird is breast side up. Use a carving fork (if you have one; if not, a regular one will do) to hold the bird steady.

3   Put the carving knife between the body and the leg and gently slide up and down until you can remove the drumstick and thigh in one piece – you can separate them after this if you prefer (**6**). Repeat on the other side.

4   Remove the wings.

5   Now carve each breast in turn, holding the knife at a slight angle and aiming to cut slices around 5mm thick.

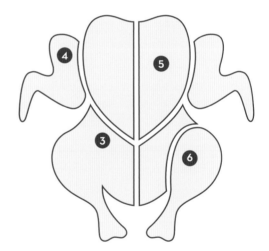

Stop your mouth burning when you've eaten something spicy

The obvious thing to do when you've eaten something spicy and your mouth is on fire is to reach for a cold glass of water. But actually, that's the worst thing you can do.

When the kids decided to eat some of my spicy sushi – which they won't be doing again in a hurry – I gave them milk to soothe their burning mouths, which did the trick. Here are some other things you can try too:

- **Yogurt**. It's no coincidence that side dishes such as raita are often served alongside the hottest curries. Chillies contain oily capsaicin, and although water will make the burning worse, casein, the protein found in milk, helps break this down and will neutralize the burn.

- **Sugar**. This can help neutralize the heat (as well as allowing the mouth to focus on a different taste). Try a teaspoonful, or use honey for the same effect.

- **Milk chocolate** – it's the dairy thing (see above).

- **Bread**. This is not only delightfully bland, but it can help to soak up the chilli oil, too.

- **Citrus** – works in a similar way to dairy.

- **Alcohol** (if appropriate); beer has been found to help, but only temporarily. It's that oil and water issue again.

When meat is safe to eat

My great fear in life is food poisoning, mainly because I've had it twice and each time it was horrific! One time it was so bad that I called an ambulance – the only time I've called an ambulance in my life. They gave me an intravenous drip because I couldn't keep anything down. It was the most debilitating feeling.

Over the course of my career I've eaten a lot of very odd things, half the time without even knowing what they were. I ate intestines when I was in Sierra Leone, and on a trip to the Yap Islands they sacrificed an animal as part of a special buffet; my job was to keep the flies away from the meat as they chopped it up in the sun. I waved my palm leaf next to a little girl who kept catching the blood from the animal with her leaf, so by the end of it we looked like something out of *Lord of the Flies* ... and then we ate it.

I've eaten the weirdest things in the weirdest places, but ironically it was minced meat in north London that took me down. A Bolognese sauce that I didn't warm up properly.

So maybe it's not surprising that since that experience I've become a living nightmare around food. Before I eat anything it's: Is this cooked through? How long did you cook this for? How many days old is it? It drives Sim mad.

There's a simple rule when it comes to cooking meat safely:

'Red meat is fine to eat when it's pink; but don't eat pink (or 'white') meat when it's red.'

However, as with any rule, there are exceptions!

• Pork joints, which look pink but are actually classified as red, can be eaten slightly underdone – but never more than that.

• Beef and lamb joints can be served rare and bloody, if that's the way you like them. Mince is another matter altogether. My ill-fated Bolognese sauce has proved that to me once and for all.

WHAT'S THE DEAL WITH MINCE?

Any harmful bacteria on meat is found on the outside. If you sear the piece/joint at a high temperature before putting it in the oven that will kill it, so it's fine to serve the meat in the centre underdone.

But when meat is minced, the bacteria from the outside is spread all the way through, which is why it's important to cook burgers, sausages, kebabs, meatballs, (and Bolognese sauce) well so there are no pink bits, it's steaming hot throughout, and the juices run clear.

Poultry (chicken and turkey) should ALWAYS be fully cooked. Any pink or red bits can have very nasty consequences. If you're not quite sure, cut into the meat at its thickest point to check (the meat should be white and not translucent and any juices should run clear), or a meat thermometer can be helpful to check the all-important internal temperature of whatever it is you're cooking.

COOKING TEMPERATURES

Chicken, pork, burgers, sausages, and mince	Must reach 75°C or above.
Lamb	Between 46°C for rare and 72°C for well done
Beef	50°C rare and 72°C well done.

HOW TO
Freeze food

Frozen food can be a lifesaver for busy families, so you've got something you can pull out of the freezer and put on the table without a fuss when you need to feed everyone quickly. Batch-cooking then freezing a few recipes is also well worth doing, as it means you can have a fantastic home-cooked, healthy meal on the table in minutes.

However, my fear of food poisoning definitely comes into play when it comes to using the freezer, because I'm always worried that I will get it wrong. It's not like I don't know what to do, but my Bolognese sauce episode has scarred me deeply. I follow all the guidelines: I let the food cool to room temperature before I put it into the freezer, then I start worrying that something has gone wrong, and I get this ridiculous fear. So then I think I shouldn't freeze it because I'm going to freeze all the germs inside it! For someone who really should be able to understand this, it seems I don't really understand it at all. (I'm the same with rice too: I'm nervous as I know that if that's not handled properly and allowed to cool quickly and thoroughly, it can mean bad bacteria forms and lead to another bout of food poisoning!)

Sim is the opposite. He will freeze stuff all day long. This chicken's about to go off? Not a problem, I'll freeze it. He's right, of course, and the freezer is the ideal way to avoid food waste. So we now have an agreement that he should just go ahead and do it and not tell me any of the details!

So, for those of us who need a bit more reassurance and guidance, this is how to freeze food correctly (and safely!):

- Make sure your freezer is set at the right temperature: 0°F or -18°C.

- Freeze food as soon as you can after buying or cooking it, but never put warm or hot food in – wait until it's fully cooled or you will raise the temperature of the freezer, which could compromise everything else that is in there. It also means higher energy bills as your freezer has to work harder to get back down to the right temperature again.

- Wrap food well before freezing, otherwise it could end up with freezer burn. This won't harm you, but it doesn't look terribly appealing – you'll see it as white marks where the food has got dehydrated when it has been exposed to air.

- Label it! Unless you fancy a game of freezer roulette whereby you end up defrosting something very different to what you thought you'd taken out for dinner (I remember when the dahl turned out to be stewed apple). It's remarkable how samey many foods can look when they are frozen.

- For shop-bought food, follow the guidance on the packet regarding how long it should be frozen for. Some foods are fine to be left in the freezer for months on end, but others should be eaten much sooner or the quality will start to deteriorate.

- Beware refreezing! It's fine to take out a raw ingredient, defrost it, cook it, and then refreeze the cooked and cooled dish, but you should absolutely avoid refreezing a previously frozen cooked dish, or refreezing defrosted raw ingredients. So you could freeze raw mince, defrost it, make a Bolognese sauce and then freeze that, but you can't defrost a Bolognese sauce and then refreeze any leftovers, or defrost the mince and refreeze any that you haven't used.

- If you are freezing a large amount of food, divide it into smaller portions. If you've got enough soup for six but only want to feed two people, chipping away at a large block trying to get the amount you want is fruitless (and dangerous, with a high potential for injury!).

- Defrost food properly before cooking it. Some things are fine cooked straight from the freezer (again, be guided by manufacturers' labels), but never cook raw chicken or larger joints of meat until they have been fully defrosted first. Eat within 24 hours of defrosting and always make sure the food is steaming hot throughout.

UNIDENTIFIED FROZEN OBJECTS
Even though we try to rotate what's in the freezer so nothing is left frozen for too long, somehow there's always a Magnum stuck to the back of it and the odd thing that seems to have been in there forever. My breast milk is still in there because I know what I went through to get it and I can't bring myself to throw it out!

Boil the perfect egg

'Can't even boil an egg' is often used as a slur to indicate that someone can't cook. It's an interesting choice of expression – I mean, we can *all* boil an egg. You just stick it in a pan of water. But boiling the *perfect* egg is different.

Different – but not difficult, as long as you follow these steps:

1   If you keep your eggs in the fridge, take them out in advance and leave them to reach room temperature before cooking.

2   Bring a saucepan of water to a rolling boil.

3   Put the eggs in – it's best not to drop them in as they may crack; instead, lower them into the water using a spoon.

4   Cook for 4-5 minutes if you're after a dippy egg. If you're after a firmer yolk (to chop up for a Niçoise salad or suchlike), leave them for an extra couple of minutes and then put them straight into cold water to stop them cooking any longer.

While this method gives perfect results every time, I confess my own approach is often a little laissez-faire. I generally put the eggs in a pan of cold water and wait for it to boil before starting the timer, and it's a bit hit and miss, so I think it's fair to argue there is a better way of doing it and I should really go with the advice above!

STOP THE WITCHES!
Many people have a tradition of turning the empty eggshell upside down in the egg cup and smashing it 'so the witches can't sail in it'. Whether you believe this or not, it can be very satisfying to do – and kids love it.

Understand alcohol

～

Understanding alcohol and having limits is something that many people think is only relevant for older teenagers and young adults, but it's worth bearing in mind that in the UK it's legal for a child aged 5 plus to be given alcohol at home. (Though as the charity Drinkaware points out, this doesn't mean it's recommended.)

And although it's against the law for anyone under 18 to buy alcohol (or for an adult to buy it on their behalf – unless it's beer, wine, or cider for a child aged over 16 when eating a table meal in licensed premises), teens have been finding ways to drink at parties since time began and that's not likely to change any time soon.

So educating your child and empowering them with the knowledge of what's what is the best way to keep them safe. To me, it's hugely important that my kids understand the consequences of drinking alcohol – and also how massively drinks can vary in their potency and alcohol content. That said, thinking responsibly about alcohol is important at any age, and it's a useful refresher for adults, too. It's all too easy to down a glass of wine that someone hands you without thinking about how many units it might contain. (Bear in mind that the MAXIMUM units recommended for an adult over an entire week are fourteen.)

So here are a few key points about alcohol that are worth sharing:

1   Alcohol is measured in units. Units are based on how strong the drink is and NOT how much liquid you are getting: a pint of beer and a pint of vodka are VERY different prospects.

2   Different people react very differently to alcohol – your gender, height, size, build, and tolerance to it can all play a part in how quickly it affects you.

3   Just because something looks like water or is mixed with fruit juice doesn't mean it is not extremely powerful.

Continued overleaf →

4   Know your measures. I show the girls how a shot glass can contain the same amount of alcohol as a large beer glass. They can't get their heads around that, so I get them to pour a tequila shot, or two measures of gin, or a glass of wine, and then line them up in order to demonstrate exactly how it works. If you think that a pint of beer may contain around three units, but a pint of vodka would contain around twenty-three, it's a really effective way to demonstrate this! There's a massive lesson in that. And it really matters.

5   **One unit can be:**

| 250ml | 25ml | 250ml | 76ml |

Half a pint of lower-strength (4%) lager/beer or cider

A single measure of spirits (40%)

Most of a small alcopop (4%)

Less than a small glass of wine (13%)

Bear in mind that the measures many pubs and bars now serve are larger than that and can be up to two units. Also measures poured at home tend to be more random or generous than a single unit.

When it comes to wine, it is also good to know that bars and restaurants often serve large glasses (250ml). Just one of these can be the equivalent of up to a third of a standard bottle – which is three or more units. A 330ml bottle of lager is around 1.7 units.

'A pint of beer may contain around three units, but a pint of vodka would contain around twenty-three!'

TRUTH AND DARES

There are some ridiculous – and really dangerous – dares going around at the moment. On TikTok I have seen games where people try to down as much of a bottle of vodka as they can. I showed this to the girls and told them hands down it was FAKE. When Ava said, 'No, no, they can really drink it – I saw them,' I told her, 'Trust me, baby girl, that's not real. It's water – otherwise they would be dead.' Explaining that what they see on social media is often not real and, more importantly, really dangerous and deceptive, particularly in relation to alcohol, is SO important.

BEWARE A WOLF IN SHEEP'S CLOTHING!

Banning alcohol isn't going to be effective with teens. Remember, if it's something they want to do, they will find a way whatever, because nothing is more appealing than forbidden fruit. My view is that these things soon lose their allure when they are allowed, within reason, under parental supervision, so there's a good argument for letting your kids have their first drink at home with you.

When your kids reach an age at which you are happy for them to try alcohol, it's important to remind them that looks and taste can be hugely deceptive. Those brightly coloured cocktails you get on holiday may taste like fruit and look like a slushy, but they can also be lethal, and one glass may well take you above your quota and what you can actually tolerate. It's the same with alcopops, which can slip down as easily as any other fizzy drink so you don't realize until too late that you have had way too much. Again, it's hugely important to me to empower my kids with this knowledge.

IGNORE THE TAUNTS

We've all heard it.

'Have a proper drink. You're so boring. You're such a lightweight.'

But the message is to never, ever allow yourself to be pressured into drinking more than you feel comfortable (or anything at all) by other people. As a teen, or even as an adult, there is NO shame in not wanting to drink, not liking how it makes you feel, not liking the taste, not wanting to keep up with others. Make sure your kids know that alcohol can be really dangerous – if their friends seem to be asleep, or possibly unconscious, they should always call for help, as they might be in real trouble. And in an age when everything is recorded, remind them too that any videos and pics of drunken behaviour will last far longer than their hangover.

13

Clean living

Up early. Hero, aged 8, and Ava, aged 12. On beach clean-up duty

↑

'It's not as good as
Peppa Pig.' Hero aged 4,
and Ava aged 8

Read a washing label

Okay, I confess. When it comes to laundry symbols I know the main ones, but some of the others are a little sketchy, which is why I'm as guilty as the next person when it comes to shrinking things or turning them a different colour.

That said, most of the things I have shrunk are my fiancé's jumpers, which then fit me perfectly, so it's not always such a bad thing.

Trying to fit the laundry into the 1,001 other things that need doing is challenge enough without having to wrestle with the tiny hieroglyphics on a standard clothes label. So many of them look the same that it's no wonder that we end up just bunging stuff into the washing machine and hoping for the best. However, I have learned the hard way that playing roulette with washing labels is not a great idea at all. So here's your guide to remembering what's what without having to resort to Google every time you put a wash on. And without turning yet another of your white shirts pink.

These are generally about machine washing. One line underneath means permanent press/minimum iron (no, nor me); two, you should use a gentle or delicates programme; and the one that's crossed out means do not wash at all. The one with the hand is – no shock here – hand wash only.

Unsurprisingly, these refer to ironing instructions (who'd have thought?). The dots correspond with those on most irons but, essentially: one is low temperature; two medium; and three high. Again, if it's crossed out then it's an 'avoid this altogether' thing.

Triangles for some reason are all about bleach. The blank one means it's fine to pop some bleach into your laundry; the crossed-out one means it is a very bad idea indeed; and the one with the lines in it means non-chlorine bleach is okay.

These are about choosing the correct temperature for tumble dryers, which is important if you don't want to shrink your clothes. The circle in the square means the item can be tumble-dried, and dots are much the same as the ones on the iron (low, medium, and high). The crossed-out one means put the item in there at your peril – it's unlikely to end well.

If your item can't be tumble-dried, it's back to more traditional ways of drying. If the square has a drooping line, it means line dry – so you can hang these outside to dry. Three vertical lines means drip dry on a rack indoors or outside, whereas the horizontal line means dry flat, which is important for clothes like woollen jumpers that might stretch and lose their shape if they are hung up.

If an item can't be washed by hand or machine, it might have a dry clean label on it. The empty circle means it is fine to dry clean, whereas the crossed-out circle means definitely don't dry clean.

Never ignore the numbers: Don't be tempted to think 'Oh, this is cotton, I can wash it at a much higher temperature than the one on the label'. The instructions will also take into account colours (which can bleed, run, or fade), as well as buttons, sequins, and embroidery which can be damaged or destroyed if washed at the wrong temperature or shoved in the tumble dryer.

HOW TO
Do the laundry

I have a blended family of seven. That's a lot of laundry. As my toddler loves playing in the mud and spilling breakfast down himself and my girls love dance and sport, I genuinely think my washing machine is the one thing I couldn't actually live without. It's forever on the go. I taught my girls to do laundry at an early age, as when you're young, most chores seem like a game. Putting clothes into piles and watching them spin doesn't seem like work when you're little. If they need something washed urgently, they can now pop it in the machine themselves, and I'll dry and iron. It mostly runs smoothly, although I draw the line at matching and balling socks. That's a Saturday job for the girls ... and my toddler!

MY GOLDEN RULES OF LAUNDRY

1   Separate dry cleaning from what can go in the washing machine.

2   Split that laundry pile into darks and lights, taking note of anything that needs to be washed at a lower temperature, or uses the handwash or delicates programmes.

3   If something is particularly dirty – covered in mud (or worse), for example – it should be washed separately from everything else. Take towels and sheets out of the equation, though, as they can generally be washed at a higher temperature than most clothes.

4   It's worth treating any stubborn marks with a stain remover before adding them to the machine. Note that some items of clothing advise that they should be washed inside out – this helps to protect certain finishes, such as embroidery, sequins, or beading.

5   If you are using a liquid tablet, you should chuck that in before you add the clothes. For powder or solid tablets, follow the instructions on the packet.

'ALWAYS check the pockets of clothes before you add them to the machine!'

6   Make sure you choose the right programme (see above). Most clothes can be washed perfectly well at 30°C – and washing at lower temperatures also helps in terms of energy saving, too. Unless you are washing wool or delicate items, or things that specify handwashing or other special care, a regular cycle will be fine.

7   ALWAYS check the pockets of clothes before you add them to the machine, as there may be items within them that might get damaged in the wash. Or stray tissues – which means everything will come out covered in bits of white fluff, which are a nightmare to remove.

8   Do up any zips and buttons – this helps prevent fastenings snagging on other fabrics and making holes.

9   Don't overfill the machine – nothing will clean properly and you may break it.

10 Unload the machine and hang everything up as soon as the cycle is finished. This helps prevent creasing and avoids that nasty musty smell that they take on when things have been left in a damp heap for too long.

So, teach these simple rules to your kids to set up them for life. Even better, once they know how to do their own washing there can be no more arguments about why their sports kit or favourite top/jeans are not clean when they need them!

Remove common stains

There are times when your clothes get marks on them that make your heart sink, but thankfully some of the worst offenders can be removed to leave your clothes as good as new – if you act quickly and know what to do.

POLLEN

One of my favourite laundry hacks is for removing pollen. Somehow you only have to look at a bunch of lilies and it's everywhere, and it can stain horribly.

The golden rule here is NEVER rub it – that will simply push the powder deeper into the weave of the fabric, making it even more difficult to remove. Don't wet it either, as that will just spread the stain. The best solution? Grab a piece of Sellotape, press down and, hey presto, gone! You can also use the narrow (crevice) nozzle on your vaccum cleaner to the same effect.

MAKE-UP

How badly this stains varies depending on the product. As ever, it's good to test methods on a small area of the item before giving it a go on the stain in a more visible place. For powder, blusher, and similar, first blow away any excess (carefully) using a hairdryer on a cool setting. Then dab gently with make-up remover on a piece of cotton wool. For mascara, dab the area with washing-up liquid on a clean cloth, and for lipstick, use rubbing alochol, applied gently using cotton wool.

NAIL POLISH

Put the item in a freezer bag and pop it into the freezer, or you can put an ice pack on the mark for this, then once really cold, dab the stain carefully with nail-polish remover.

MUD

Let it dry and brush as much of it off as you can – an old toothbrush is ideal for this. Soak for 15–20 minutes in lukewarm water mixed with either a stain remover or a biological washing powder or liquid. Machine-wash as normal (using biological powder or liquid).

BLOOD

A useful one, especially if you have kids with a propensity for acquiring grazes and scrapes (looking at you, Hero), or who get regular nosebleeds, as I used to. There are a few things you can try:

- **Cold water**, which helps the blood to break down – never hot. Remove as much of the blood as you can and rinse the stain on both sides of the fabric. Try to keep the water/blood mix just to the affected area rather than spreading it further.

- **White vinegar**. Pour a little directly onto the stain, rub it in gently with a clean cloth, then machine-wash as normal.

- **Salt**. Dissolve some salt in cold water and sponge the stain carefully with this mix until it disappears. Saline solution works in the same way.

- **Milk**. Soak the stain with some milk for several hours, then rinse in cold water and machine-wash as normal.

- **Bicarbonate of soda**. Blend one part bicarb with two parts water to form a paste. Dab this onto the stain and leave for 30 minutes before wiping away any residue and then washing as normal.

- **Aspirins**. Crush two and mix with water. Soak the stain with this mix for 30 minutes, then rinse.

- **Lemon and salt**. Cut the lemon in two and rub the cut side over the stain, then sprinkle salt over the affected area. Leave for 10 minutes then dab away any excess before washing as normal.

- If the stain has already dried, try to scrape off any excess – but don't use anything sharp, as it will damage the fabric – then apply cold water to loosen.

- You can also try using a specially formulated bloodstain remover.

If you are using anything other than water on your stain, check the fabric label first and try a test patch where it won't be noticed, to make sure the colour is not affected.

INK

If you have rubbing alcohol, put a little on some cotton wool. If you don't, you can use an alcohol-based hand gel – and we all have plenty of that these days! – instead. Dab this onto the stain, taking care not to rub it in. Let it soak in for up to half an hour. Wash on as hot a wash as you can (check those labels again!) using a biological washing powder or tablet.

Iron a shirt

I love ironing. I know it's not for everyone, but I find it relaxing and it gives me time to listen to music or make phone calls. I haven't let the younger kids loose with the iron yet – they're a bit too young – although I have got Ava started. But I have shown them how to get creases out without an iron – something I have learned from the wardrobe experts I've met in studios over the years.

GETTING STEAMY

On most of the photoshoots I've done they use a steamer rather than an iron and it works brilliantly. To do this at home, either boil the kettle and use the steam from that (which can obviously be hot, so be careful!) or hang up your clothes in the bathroom and turn the shower on. Then while you're getting clean your clothes will be steaming beautifully and dropping creases – perfectly killing two birds with one stone.

If you want to indulge in a more traditional shirt pressing, there are a few things to consider for perfect presentation.

How hot should the iron be? Check the label on the shirt, but generally a hot iron is fine on a cotton or linen shirt, and definitely not fine on man-made fibres such as polyester, or delicate fabrics like silk and wool.

Remember:
- Polyester and silk
- •• Wool or viscose
- ••• Cotton or linen

'I love ironing. I know it's not for everyone, but I find it relaxing and it gives me time to listen to music or make phone calls.'

Then what? Make sure you've undone all the buttons and get ironing. Follow this order for a crease-free shirt:

1. Start with the collar. Do the underside first, then work from the edge to the middle.

2. Next, do the shoulder panel on the back. The narrow end of the board is good for this bit.

3. Cuffs are next. Again, start on the inside first.

4. Put the sleeves lengthwise along the board and press from shoulder to cuff.

5. Iron on the wrong side of the button band – lots of buttons don't work well with direct heat – again working from top to bottom.

6. Next, iron the front panels. Like the sleeves, lie them along the board and go from top to bottom.

7. Finally, iron the rest of the back of the shirt, below the shoulder panel.

HOW TO
Clean shoes

As a Navy brat, I have a real thing about clean shoes – I notice the shine immediately. But after finding polish all over my skirting boards when I got the girls to do their own, I'm now the one who does them all in our house.

TRAINERS

Many brands advocate against just sticking them in the washing machine (although I'm a fan), but if you'd rather play it safe try one of these methods instead:

- Use a shoe brush or an old toothbrush to remove any dirt and remove the laces from the shoe.

- Wash the soles (and midsoles) using warm water mixed with a little washing powder/liquid. Use a soft brush to clean any crevices. Dry using a soft cloth.

- Clean the upper part of the shoe using more of the above solution and a soft cloth – you don't want to scratch as you clean. Use a microfibre or other soft cloth to blot dry and repeat if needed.

- Wash the laces by rubbing in some of the warm water/laundry detergent solution. Rinse, then dry with a soft cloth.

- Leave everything to dry at room temperature.

The last point is very important. When I was 14 I saved up for a pair of trainers I desperately wanted. My mum put them in the washer ... and then the dryer. When I opened my PE bag, I found two tiny elf shoes. I was devastated.

CANVAS/FABRIC SHOES (SUCH AS PLIMSOLLS, PUMPS, SANDALS)

1   Avoid the washing machine – this is likely to affect the glue that keeps the shoe together.

2   First, remove any surface mud or dirt using a dry tea towel or paper towel.

3   Use an old toothbrush dipped in a solution of one teaspoon washing-up liquid and two cups of warm water to gently scrub the fabric, trying not to get it too wet. Do one section of the shoe at a time, but make sure you treat each equally to avoid any patching. You should work with the grain of the fabric, not against it.

4   Moisten a paper towel with cold water and use it to blot the shoe clean and remove any detergent. Repeat as needed.

5   Gently blot the shoe with a dry paper towel and dry away from sunlight or direct heat sources.

LEATHER

1   Remove the laces and get rid of any dirt or dust with a brush or cloth.

2   Apply a coloured wax polish (beeswax helps the leather last longer) in small circular movements all over the leather, then leave it to absorb for at least 20 minutes.

3   Buff with a soft brush or cloth to enhance the shine.

SUEDE

1   Only clean suede when it is dry, to prevent damaging the fibres.

2   To protect the soft grain, use a special suede cleaning brush to get rid of dust and dirt. Brush in the direction of the grain.

3   Remove any stubborn marks with a rubber – you can use a special suede rubber, or just a common or garden one purloined from a handy pencil case.

4   If all else fails, use a little white vinegar on a cloth and rub it back and forth on the fabric. The moisture will make the suede look darker initially, but when it's dry the normal colour will return.

Dry out wet shoes

Oh, the excitement of buying my son his first ever pair of proper shoes! He wanted to go straight to the park to try them out ... then he spent the entire time walking through the deepest puddles he could find. By the end of our outing, the shoes couldn't have been any wetter had he worn them in the bath, but thankfully I knew how to rescue them so they weren't written off after just one wear.

Whether you've been caught in the rain, soaked by a stray wave on the beach, or been overexuberant when washing the car, drying out shoes is something that's always worth doing properly, otherwise they will end up mouldy and/or smelly.

There are various things you can do to avoid this:

- My favourite method is stuffing the shoes with balled-up newspaper (push it right down into the toes). This will absorb some of the moisture and speed up the drying process. If the shoes aren't dry after a couple of hours, replace the damp newspaper with fresh, dry paper.

- Use a hairdryer – although this is best in emergencies only, as the heat can damage the shoe.

- Wrap the shoes in newspaper and put them somewhere warm, but not directly next to a heat source. Beware of print coming off on light-coloured shoes – for those, try wrapping them in kitchen roll or a clean tea towel instead. If the shoes have removable insoles, always take them out and let them dry separately, to speed things up.

- Pop the shoes in a box of rice. The trick that works wonders on phones that have fallen out of your back pocket into the loo can also do the job for footwear.

Get chewing gum out of clothes

It's not just slime that is banned in my house, chewing gum makes the list, too. I don't need to explain why this is the case to anyone who has had the joy of trying to get either of those things out of carpets and hair. I've done the whole trying to brush it out thing, and in the end the only thing that's worked is scissors. It's not pretty. So, no more gum.

Getting gum on clothes is harder to avoid when people leave it around the place and you end up sitting on it, on benches and public transport. So if you're unlucky enough to find some stuck to your clothes, here's how to get rid of it:

1   Freeze it. Either put the garment in a plastic bag and pop it into the freezer for a couple of hours until the gum is frozen solid, or if that's not possible, rub an ice cube over the affected area instead. If you are folding the clothing, make sure the gummy bit doesn't make contact with any other, unaffected part of the fabric, or it will stick together and make it doubly hard to get it off.

2   Remove the solidified gum gently, especially if the garment is delicate. Rather than just pulling and hoping for the best, ease it off carefully.

3   If there are any small bits left after doing this you can remove them using heat – obviously exercising caution if it's a delicate fabric like silk. Pop your hairdryer on medium to warm the gum very gently, then remove with care.

4   For less-delicate fabrics you can also use an iron. Lay the gummy side on a piece of clean cardboard and use a medium heat to press the reverse of the fabric. Don't be tempted to turn up the heat; patience is key. It may take a few minutes but eventually the gum should stick to the cardboard, then you can peel the clothing away carefully and launder in the usual manner.

Recycle

When I was a child this was something none of us thought about, so we have had to learn about it as adults instead. For the kids who have grown up with the idea of recycling, it's the norm, but reinforcing why it matters is important, to encourage all generations to do their bit for the planet. Showing kids that they can do their bit by recycling can make a huge impact. It also leads onto litter picking, playground pick-up, and beach clean-ups (we even join these when we go on holiday).

We have a very strict recycling policy at work and one particular person gets very upset when people put the wrong cups into the dry recycling. But my sister did work experience at a recycling plant and she told me that if one thing that shouldn't be there infiltrates the bin, then the whole lot is ruined. You might think there is no problem with popping in a used plastic bottle, for example, but if it's covered in food residue then it can't be recycled. Learning this has really made me take stock and think about what I recycle and how.

So, on that note:

- Check what your local council does and doesn't take – there's no point filling your bin and including something they don't accept. Then the whole lot will end up in landfill.

- Cutting down on single-use plastics is hugely important. Choose paper or glass containers where possible and keep reusable shopping bags handy to avoid having to keep buying carrier bags.

- Wash out empty jars, pots, and tins before they go into the recycling bin.

- Crush empty plastic bottles before you recycle, then screw the lids back on. Leave lids on jars, too.

- They might be made of cardboard, but greasy takeaway containers such as pizza boxes CAN'T be recycled, because once the grease is soaked in, it can't be removed.

- Most products now have information on the packaging to say which parts can/can't be recycled, so read it carefully before you throw it out.

- Most paper can be recycled – but tissues, kitchen roll, wipes, foil-based wrapping paper, tissues, sticky labels, and Post-it notes can't and should go in the bin instead.

- Large and non-recyclable items should be disposed of at the local tip.

- Lots of businesses are waking up to the need for sustainable packaging and you can do your bit by supporting them. Conversely, if products you buy use a load of unnecessary packaging, why not question the company about why they do this? Speaking up can force positive change.

Recently, I learned about a great garbage patch in the Pacific Ocean that is made up of floating rubbish and plastic particles (or microplastics) that come from items including old toothbrushes to water bottles, plastic bags, and old mobile phones. None of these ever fully break down, so together all this is creating what *National Geographic* describes as 'a cloudy soup intermixed with larger items such as fishing gear and shoes'.[1]

Estimates reckon that this 'patch' covers an area of up to twice the size of Texas.[2] That's 1.5 million km^2 and yet I'd never heard of it or read anything about it until now. You'd think it would be front-page news. The effect of this on marine life is catastrophic and the sheer size of it is utterly shocking, clearly illustrating the extent of what we've been doing to our planet. It's essential to remember that even small actions can be important.

1 https://www.nationalgeographic.org/encyclopedia/great-pacific-garbage-patch/

2 https://www.pbs.org/newshour/science/the-great-pacific-garbage-patch-weighs-more-than-43000-cars-and-is-way-bigger-than-previously-thought

14

Handy hints

Me, aged 3, on my dad's ship's telephone. M is for Mike. Y is for Yankee...

Full geek mode (got to love a planet though)

ALMHOUSES: Statue decayed at the Fishermens Hospital, Yarmouth. Picture taken April 1981. REF c12488

LOOK LEFT: Green on November 10, 198

KLASS ACT: St Marys RC School pupils go through to the final of the Meccano Young Technologist of the Year contest, including Myleene Klass. December 1988. REF c11192

Making a fire in Sweden

On-site checks

I've got packing a bag down to a fine art — roll everything!

How to make a bed every day, Ava-style, aged 7

HOW TO

Remember people's names

You are introduced to a group of people and then later find yourself having to introduce one of them to someone else and you can't for the life of you remember their name. This is VERY easily done and it's mortifying for all involved.

So, how do you avoid offending people by scrabbling around for their name ... and then getting it wrong?

Easy! Use their name to their face at every opportunity. It's a trick I learned long ago and it really works. So if you are introduced to Jane, you respond by saying things like:

- Hello, Jane.
- Lovely to meet you, Jane.
- Jane, how do you know so and so?
- Ava, this is Jane. Jane, Ava plays the piano and the cello.

You can also keep repeating it (in your head though, otherwise the conversation is likely to be pretty brief!) while you chat. If you are meeting several people at once, focus on one at a time or the task will be impossible!

Try to find a cue that you can link to their name – even if it's oblique. It works, honestly. So you might remember a lofty person named Paul by dubbing him (again, silently) 'tall Paul'. Brian might have a beard that looks more like a mane (Brian the lion). Clare, blonde, could become Clare with the fair hair. The possibilities are endless but once you've mastered the art it won't let you down.

Pluck a name out of the ether if you've forgotten what someone is called. It's far better to own it (I'm so sorry, I've forgotten your name) than call them the wrong thing. The same applies if someone calls you by the wrong name. Correct them politely. It's awkward, but it's much easier than letting it go on for ages and them then wondering why you never said anything sooner.

246

HOW TO

Roll up fairy lights

Anyone who has spent hours trying to unravel strings of lights that have just been dumped in a box or bag and left for a year will agree that this is a life skill worth knowing. Never underestimate the joy of just unrolling them when you need them, with not a knot in sight.

And it couldn't be easier.

- Take a cardboard tube (the inside of a kitchen roll or roll of wrapping paper are perfect) or make a tube from rolled newspaper.

- Coil the lights round it.

- Done!

Tip – *a Pringles (or equivalent) tube also works perfectly for this. And you get to eat the crisps first.*

Remember the phonetic alphabet

F for Freddie, S for sugar … this is my pet hate; a made-up phonetic alphabet! There's always someone who'll say this and it gets me every time. Apart from anything else, the phonetic alphabet is an international one, so 'S for sugar' is meaningless when talking to someone from Spain (*azucar*) or Italy (*zucchero*) or Malaysia (*gula*). You get the point.

As my dad was in the Navy, the phonetic alphabet was something he used all the time. I'd hear him across the radios, and when you're a kid and hear what sounds like a whole new language, it's magical. Dad also used to watch *Juliet Bravo* and all the other classic Eighties cop shows where we'd hear them spell things out like this and think how cool and sophisticated it sounded. I'm sure at some point as a child I would have used F for Freddie and been corrected, and I've never forgotten it since.

With my own kids we broke this up and used rhythm to help them remember the phonetic alphabet, so that they could also enjoy the sound and feel of it.

*A*lpha *B*ravo	*C*harlie *D*elta
*E*cho *F*oxtrot	*G*olf *H*otel
*I*ndia *J*uliet	*K*ilo *L*ima
*M*ike *N*ovember	*O*scar *P*apa
*Q*uebec *R*omeo	*S*ierra *T*ango
*U*niform *V*ictor	*W*hisky *X*-ray
*Y*ankee *Z*ulu	

Practising in everyday situations also helps. I encourage them to use it to read out numberplates or spell out their names and see who can do it fastest – that way you soon find yourself using it naturally when someone asks you to spell something out. The kids love it and get really excited by it, and it makes me very happy that, in a situation where she needs to spell something out clearly, the days of hearing my younger daughter saying, 'Uh, H for … Hula Hoops? E for … elephant. R for … um …'are over!

Handle sparklers safely

Although sparklers are usually reserved for firework displays and ad-hoc celebrations, they are an entry point into how we look after ourselves and our children around fire and crowds from a young age. All year long, we spend our time being really wary and careful of open flames then, on one night of the year, we throw caution to the wind!

This is the easiest hack ever, but one of the best I have. Learn this and you'll be a hero at every fireworks display! Here's how:

1   Get your sparklers.

2   Raid the vegetable drawer in the fridge. You're ideally looking for a carrot or a cucumber, but I've seen parents use parsnips and potatoes.

3   Insert the end of your sparkler into the carrot lengthways. *Et voilà!* A carrot sparkler! It's sturdy for little hands to hold and far safer than waving tiny sparkler sticks around, as we all know how flimsy they can be.

4   Get your little ones to pop their used sparklers, end-first, into a bucket of sand or even water.

The best ideas are often the simplest!

TOP FIRE BRIGADE SAFETY REGULATIONS ON SPARKLERS

Most of the year, it is illegal to set off fireworks (including sparklers) between 11 p.m. and 7 a.m.

For Bonfire Night, however, the curfew is midnight and for New Year's Eve, Diwali, and Chinese New Year the cut-off is 1 a.m.

- Only buy products which carry the CE mark
- Keep them in a closed package and use them one at a time
- Don't leave sparklers unattended
- Don't put sparklers in pockets and never throw them
- Direct any sparklers well away from spectators.

Remember telephone numbers

In this age of mobile phones we have probably all become far too reliant on having every number we could ever need at our fingertips. But having them all saved on our technology can lull us into a false sense of security. If the phone is lost or stolen, runs out of battery, or we are out without it, then we're all out of speed-dial options.

I used to be brilliant with numbers and now I'm not, but what I have done is drill my kids into remembering my phone number from a very early age. Knowing how to get hold of a parent if children are lost or in trouble is so important. My girls don't know any other phone numbers as their phone usually dials for them, so knowing my number has been great for when they have really needed it. That said, it's very useful for adults to know a couple of key numbers off by heart, too. We are all far too reliant on scrolling through our contacts list to find whatever we need.

My advice for teaching them how to remember a phone number? Turn it into a song. The rhythm will help it stick in their heads far more easily. You can use any familiar tune that you know well, or make one up.

Most memory experts suggest breaking longer numbers down into smaller sections of three or four digits. It's a lot easier to remember three groups of three or four than eleven numbers in a row, just as it's much easier to remember four lines of a song than a single, longer piece of text. Take your numbers and your tune, fit them together, and sing it to yourself whenever you get the chance. It will soon become an anthem you never forget.

For toddlers/very young children, write your phone number on a wristband and put it on them when out in busy places. Teach them to point to it. Hopefully, they will never use it, but it feels better to have a way someone can contact you if needed.

Make the bed

I remember my Austrian grandmother – the same grandmother that sewed up my jeans (see page 263) – saying to me, 'Myleena, you make the bed like a sausage.' She was disgusted because she was all about the hospital corners. But actually, ironically, a beautifully made bed is really important to me these days and it makes me really happy.

I think this is the great divide between me and Sim; he couldn't care less. He's happy to just chuck the pillows and the cushions on. I find this shocking, and I know that if I didn't iron the sheets he wouldn't bother. My rules for bed-making are *very* different from his!

- All linen must be perfectly ironed. I'm a massive ironer. One of my friends thinks I'm a martyr, says it's a shocking disgrace, but I love the iron. I like knickers all pressed and neatly lined up, even socks. Neat crisp piles make me really happy.

- My tip for ironing sheets is to fold them first, then the creases are super sharp.

- Fitted sheets are easy to pop onto beds and avoid the need for making tidy corners, but make sure you pull them as far down as they will go. You definitely don't want them pinging off every time you turn over. Also, pull them taut. Lying on wrinkles won't do anything for a good night's sleep.

Continued overleaf →

In our house the rule is that no one is allowed to leave their room in the morning until beds are made. It's as much a part of our routine as getting dressed, brushing our teeth, and having breakfast. It starts the day in the right way, and it also makes getting into bed at night a hundred times nicer.

'Lying on wrinkles won't do anything for a good night's sleep.'

If you have flat rather than fitted sheets (or are using a top sheet under your duvet) then the art of the hospital corner is one to perfect:

1   Lie the sheet over the mattress so that the tops of both are aligned and there is an even amount of fabric hanging over each side.

2   Tuck the bottom side in between the mattress and base.

3   On the left side of the bed, take hold of the excess fabric, lift it, and place it on top of the mattress. The edge of the sheet should form a 45° angle with the corner of the mattress.

4   Hold on to the part that forms the angle and tuck in the hanging fabric.

5   Drop the corner, adjust the edge of the sheet to fit the corner of the mattress, and then tuck in firmly.

6   Repeat on the other side.

HOW TO … PUT ON A DUVET COVER

Fiddling with trying to get the duvet into each corner, shaking it around, and then realizing it's twisted up and having to start all over again is … frustrating.

There is an easier way. Place the duvet cover on the bed on top of the duvet. Work your hands inside the duvet cover, up toward the top corners. With your hands inside each corner, pick up the top two corners of the duvet and flip the cover inside out, over the top corners of the duvet. Holding on to the duvet corners again, inside the duvet cover, as well as the corresponding corners of the duvet itself, flip the cover back over the duvet, then pull the rest of the duvet cover down. Don't forget to fasten it at the bottom. Job done!

①

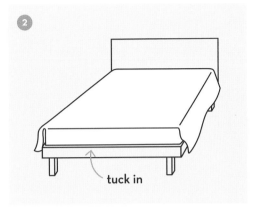

② tuck in

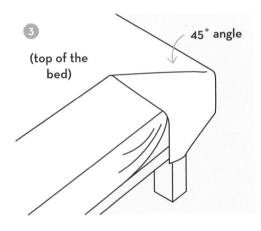

③ (top of the bed)   45° angle

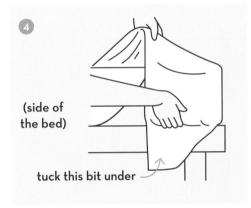

④ (side of the bed)   tuck this bit under

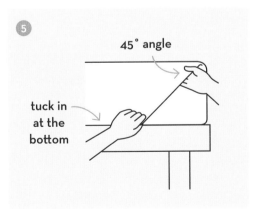

⑤ 45° angle   tuck in at the bottom

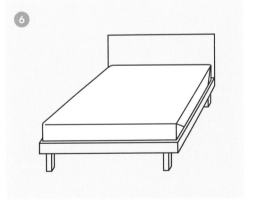

⑥

Remember how many days are in each month

Yes, you can do the whole:

Thirty days hath September,
April, June and November,
All the rest have thirty-one
Excepting February alone
And that has twenty-eight days clear
And twenty-nine in each leap year

– but I hate that rhyme (and it doesn't even rhyme!). And actually there's a much simpler way to do it that not many people seem to know about.

Knuckles!

Get someone to hold their hands out in front of them (palms down) and then clench them into fists and push them together alongside each other. Start on the furthest knuckle (on either side) for January then move to the dip next to it (February), knuckle (March), dip (April) right up to December.

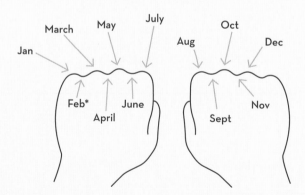

Every month that falls on a knuckle has 31 days. Every month that falls in a dip has 30, with the exception of February which, as we know, has its own rules. (There's no getting around that one.)

Back up important files

We all know how important it is to back up important documents and photos kept on your computer or online. But most of us also know how easy it is to forget to do this – at least until the worst happens. It can be truly gut-wrenching to lose something you've spent time and effort working on. And who hasn't accidentally hit the wrong button at some point, especially when you are tired? I have lost essays and scripts in exactly this way. Almost at the end, I hit one key, and that's it – I'm sitting in front of the screen in tears.

Obviously there are different ways of backing things up according to what device(s) and software you are using, but these principles are always good ones:

1   When you are working on something make sure you save it as you go along. I have a girlfriend who always says, 'Keep hitting save at regular intervals', and I have learned the hard way she is absolutely right.

2   Save things in more than one place. A friend's daughter lost her entire dissertation when, right at the end, her laptop died and none of the files could be recovered.

3   Although it's important to get into good habits to keep your files safe, a temporary measure for smaller files, such as essays, is to email them to yourself. You don't want to do this too often (or with large files), or you'll end up clogging up your inbox, but it can be a quick and useful save when needed.

4   Using an external hard drive is another option, though obviously if that gets damaged or stolen your files will go with it. Backing up online is also a good solution – there are lots of services that do this, such as iCloud, Dropbox, Google Drive, and more. Many offer a certain amount of storage for free, but if you have lots of music, photos, or other files that use up a lot of space, you will probably need to pay a small monthly fee.

5   Experts recommend the 3-2-1 rule: you should always have three copies of any important data: two 'local' (such as on different devices); and one 'off site' (or remote).

HOW TO

Tie a tie

I wore a tie for school up to the age of 15 or 16, so learning how to tie it neatly was an important skill to master.

I was taught by my dad who, being a military man, was very particular and made me tie mine using a Windsor knot. In 1980s Norfolk this was total social suicide – I was the only child in the school whose knot was bigger than Trevor McDonald's (if you're too young for this reference, look it up!). The shame.

For more traditional tie-tying there are lots of rhymes that have been devised to help children remember how to do it, although some are more oblique than others.

Try one of these:

Round and round the garden
Up the rabbit hole
Take the rabbit by its head
And tuck it down below

(The rabbit is the fat end!)

Or:
Fat over thin
Fat around again
Fat into keyhole
Right down the drain

**To tie a
simple knot:**

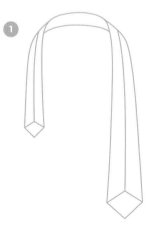

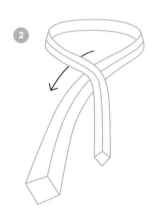

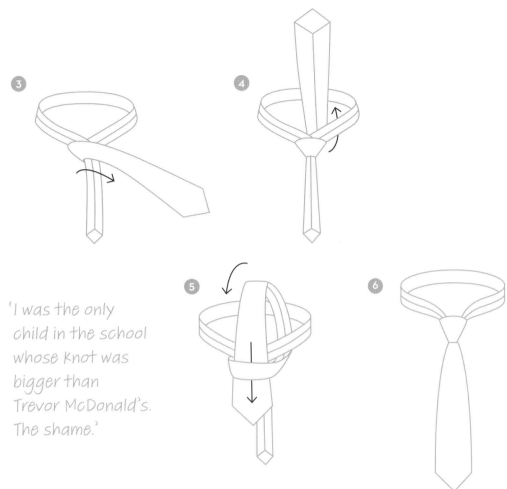

'I was the only child in the school whose knot was bigger than Trevor McDonald's. The shame.'

AND HOW TO TEACH KIDS TO TIE SHOELACES

More rhymes, more bunnies for another essential skill once they've progressed out of Velcro shoes!

Bunny ears, Bunny ears, playing by a tree.
Criss-crossed the tree, trying to catch me.
Bunny ears, Bunny ears, jumped into the hole,
Popped out the other side beautiful and bold.

Strange, but it works – this is how both Ava and Hero learned to tie their laces.

Tie knots

This is where my Navy background comes in again. I love a knot. I think I've done every single one going, but for me it's more the idea of knowing the power of what each knot can do.

My partner, Sim, also comes from a Navy background, and he and I have had long chats about our favourite knots (had to get through lockdown somehow, right?). These are our top three.

THE BOWLINE

This is a magnificent knot, like the emperor of the knot world. It's a load-bearing knot that can hold ANYTHING, but no matter how much load it's been under it's also super easy to undo. Sim and I bonded over the Bowline knot while showing our kids how to do it. I use it to get the hammock up on the balcony. It's the most important knot you'll ever learn.

To tie a Bowline:

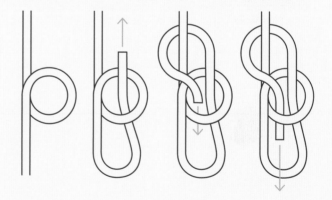

1 Make a loop near one end of your rope.

2 Pass the free end through the loop from underneath (the rabbit comes out of the hole … it's a bit like ties and shoelaces again!).

3 Wrap the end around the length of rope above the loop and pull it back down through the loop (or 'around the tree and back down the hole').

4 Hold the line and pull on the free end to tighten.

REEF (OR SQUARE) KNOT

This is a simple but effective knot whereby you just do left over right, right over left. It's really handy for joining two different types of ropes (or string) together.

To tie a Reef Knot:

1 Cross over the two ends of the rope.

2 Make a loop with one end of the rope and pass the other end through it, tucking it under and pulling it through the inside of the loop.

3 Pull the two ends of the rope together to tighten the loops and interconnect them.

THE CLOVE HITCH

Sim was all for the Sheep Bend as our final choice, but we settled on the Clove Hitch because you can use that to tow stuff, so it's really useful. It's also a simple one to learn, as essentially you make two circles and flip them, and then hook them over a tow bar.

To tie a Clove Hitch:

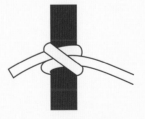

1 Wrap the end of the rope that isn't attached to whatever it is you want to tow around the pole or towing hook.

2 Take the free end and wrap it around the pole again, crossing up and over the rope underneath.

3 Slip the free end back under the crossover loop, then pull it tight to secure.

Wrap a present

Fact: wrapping something that's square or rectangular is so much easier than wrapping something that's round or curved. And that's why so many of us lump for the really simple solution for awkwardly shaped gifts: put them in a box before you wrap them!

I used to be really good at gift-wrapping but I've got lazy. I can make a present look really lovely but that requires sitting at a desk or table and being a bit organized; having your tape in a dispenser and everything close to hand. Now I'm more of a wrap-it on the-carpet-covered-in-carpet-fluff-with-Sellotape-stuck-to-my-knees person.

But there is a lovely art to it if you can give it a little time and thought. And the most important thing to remember is:

Fold, don't stick.

Fold everything, make sure it all fits really nicely, then stick the base and work from there. If you fold stick, fold stick, you can't rejiggle everything if you need to.

Here's a step-by-step guide to doing it properly (without the carpet fluff):

1   Cut the paper to size only after you've made sure it will fit comfortably around the item you're wrapping.

2   Get your bits of tape ready – better now than when you're trying to keep the paper in place and only have one free hand.

3   Put whatever you are wrapping upside down in the middle of your paper.

4   Take one side of the paper and fold it over the gift, then do the same with the opposite side, making sure they overlap where they meet.

5   Check your folds for both ends before you even think about sticking. For the open ends, flatten the top down. The sides of the paper will form triangle shapes which you then fold in so they are flat against the gift.

6   Tape securely (if it's an edge you've cut and it's not completely straight, you can always fold it over for a crisper finish).

7   Fold the bottom edge up and secure with tape.

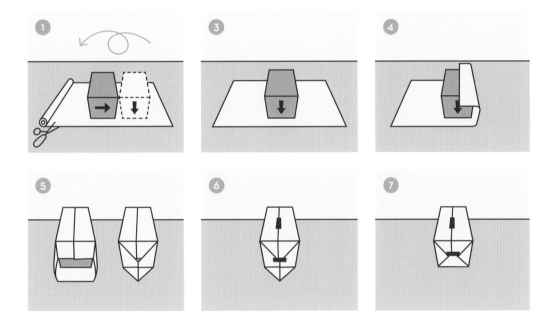

Tip – if the paper turns out to be too small when you start wrapping and so doesn't meet in the middle (and a gap showing what's inside sort of misses the point of wrapping it in the first place) rotate the gift by 45° and wrap diagonally (corner to corner) instead. A video of this hack took social media by storm, racking up more than 15 million views. Sometimes the simple solutions are the very best ones.

Mend a hole

This is something that every girl (don't get me started) used to learn as they grew up, but it rather seems to have gone out of fashion in our ever-more-disposable society.

But actually it's a great skill to have. After all, we all get holes in our clothes! I confess that I don't bother with socks, but sewing is great for mending jumpers and other larger items – and it was very handy in our house after Mothgate (see page 180)!

1   Thread your needle with wool that matches the jumper you are mending.

2   Turn the garment inside out – that way the stitching and finishing will be less visible on the 'right' side.

3   In order to help the jumper keep its shape (and to avoid sewing the front and back together by accident – easily done!) you should use a wooden darning mushroom. If you don't have one you can improvise with another curved object such as a tennis ball, or if mending a sleeve you could use a rolled-up magazine.

'If the hole is too big you may need to use a piece of fabric or iron-on interfacing to patch it before stitching.'

4   Stitch across the hole in one direction only. Don't pull too tight or you will end up with puckering or a ridged scar instead of a neatly fixed hole (again – very easily done). The trick is to leave the material as it wants to sit.

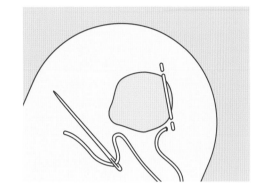

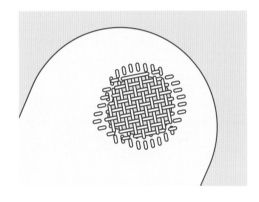

5   Weave through the stitches in the opposite direction to form a lattice or web that's secure and has no holes.

6   Fasten the yarn with a knot to keep it in place on the inside (again, don't pull too tight) and you're done!

7   If the hole is too big you may need to use a piece of fabric or iron-on interfacing (you can buy this in hardware stores or haberdashery departments) to patch it before stitching. Simply cut to fit over the hole and iron into place, or if it isn't iron-on, pin it into place. Then stitch over the fabric in exactly the same way as you do above – the fabric acts like the missing bit of fabric in the garment hole.

I learned how to sew from my mum, who used to make everything herself; I'd fall asleep to the sound of her sewing machine. Mending holes also reminds me of my Austrian granny. I remember going to stay with her and leaving my best ripped jeans hanging on a chair and when I woke up she had darned them. Every single last split. I was absolutely devastated.

Sew on a button

A small thing perhaps, but one of those skills that makes you feel invincible. Super useful and easy to do.

First things first, you need:

- a needle

- some thread that is as close to the colour of the garment/button as possible, and that matches the thread used for any other buttons too.

Threading the needle can be tricky for anyone who needs reading glasses or struggles with close vision. If that applies to you, try:

- a magnifier (if you don't have a glass then lots of smartphones have a magnifying function).

- getting a child to do it for you (all part of the learning process of course!).

- buying packs of needles with large 'eyes' or those ready threaded with cottons of various colours.

And now for the actual sewing bit:

1   Make sure you've tied a knot at the end of your thread to keep it in place when you push the needle through the garment.

Put the button exactly where you want it to end up (making sure it lines up with the corresponding buttonhole.

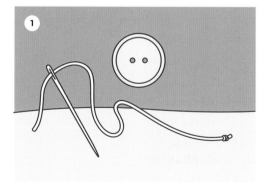

2   Push the needle up from the wrong side of the garment through the hole in the button or underneath it if it has a toggle, pulling the thread all the way through to the other side, then go down through the other hole and back through the fabric.

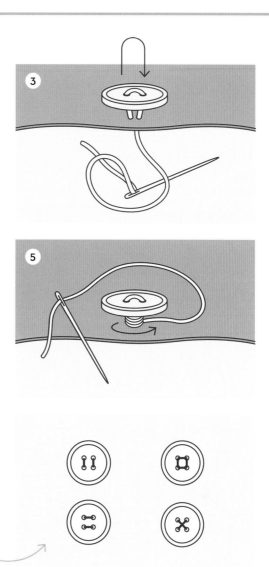

3   Repeat as needed, leaving a small gap between the button and the fabric. Don't pull the thread too tight or you won't have enough give to fit the button through the hole. I did this many a time!

4   Push the needle up through the fabric but not through the hole in the button and then wind the thread round the stitches below the button several times.

5   Push the needle back down through the fabric and make a few small stiches under the button before cutting off any excess thread (you can tie a knot too if you like, but it will hold firm without).

The process is the same for a four-hole button, but there's more variety in the stitching patterns possible. Make sure your stitching pattern matches that on the other buttons. The principles all remain the same.

I learned to do this when I was very young thanks to my Auntie Barbara who lived across the road. I liked to sew things but then I used to interrupt the adults' conversations by asking someone to tie the knot at the end. She's the one who showed me that if I just wrapped the thread underneath the button and then secured the thread below, I wouldn't need to tie a knot – and she was absolutely right.

These days, now that I design my own childrenswear, I get a lot of pleasure from choosing the details of whether it's a two- or four-hole button and whether it's cross-stitched or not – but I always remember Auntie Barbara.

Pack a suitcase

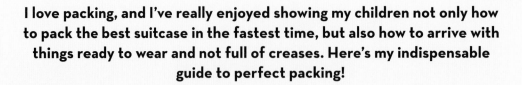

I love packing, and I've really enjoyed showing my children not only how to pack the best suitcase in the fastest time, but also how to arrive with things ready to wear and not full of creases. Here's my indispensable guide to perfect packing!

- Make a list! I love lists. I make lists for the lists, or create them just so I can have the joy of ticking things off! But it saves so much time if you know exactly what you need to take rather than having to think, do I need that? Did I already put that in?

- Simplest hack of them all: roll everything. Never fold; always roll. Not only do clothes travel far better this way – and I often don't get the chance to steam or iron things before I need to perform or work – but it's also miles easier to get them into the case.

- Put all the heavy stuff around the edges.

- Double-bag any bottles or jars containing liquid. Oh yes, I've had shampoo bottles explode and leave everything around them covered in goo. So now it's double-bagging all the way.

- Roll fabric (dresses, T-shirts) around fragile items to protect them and make sure they are cushioned on all sides. Even complex items can be rolled to maximize your space.

- Finally, add a bow/ribbon to your case handle so it's easy to identify on the conveyor belt/in the boot of the coach. Never put your full address on the case, only a phone number or email, but never your house details. Who knows where your case will end up. You don't need to alert everyone that you're not at home.

'Never fold; always roll.'

FOLD AND ROLL

Shirts, tops, and jackets:

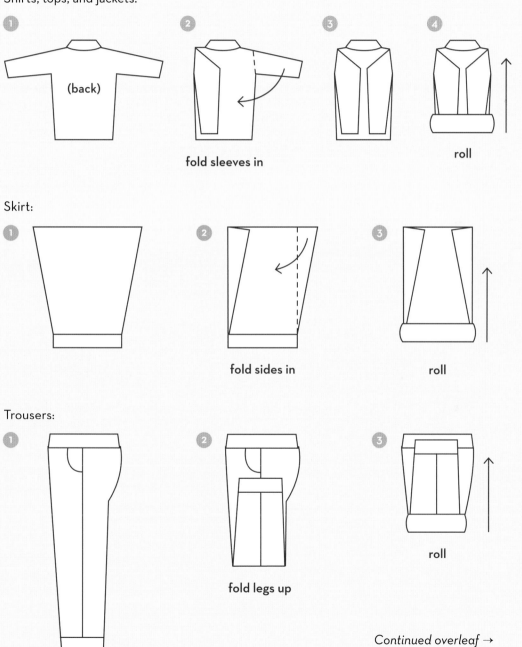

① (back)

② fold sleeves in

③

④ roll

Skirt:

① ② fold sides in ③ roll

Trousers:

① ② fold legs up ③ roll

Continued overleaf →

HAND LUGGAGE

- The obvious thing is not to take liquids in bottles over 100ml if you're going through an airport. Getting bigger bottles you've bought specially for your trip taken off you before you leave the country is heartbreaking!

- If you're travelling with small kids, take a change of clothes for you as well as them (leggings and a T-shirt take up hardly any space, but you'll thank me for it if you've been been spilled on, puked on – or worse.

- If you're going on a beach/sun holiday, have a swimsuit or bikini in the bottom of your bag. If your luggage goes astray – and, oh yes, this happens – one consolation will be that you don't have to stare miserably at the sea/pool wishing you could have a dip.

- Snacks, snacks, and more snacks. Delays, mistakes with meals ordered, meals that the kids won't eat ... the list goes on. Grumpy, hungry kids are not what you need.

In short, my motto for travelling – especially with kids – is **be prepared**. I learned to be an efficient packer from bitter experience; I have lost my luggage many a time. The worst time of all was when I was travelling alone with the girls. By the time we got to Portugal my bags had gone missing. We then flew on to America and when we got there I discovered they hadn't just lost my bags, but they'd lost my pram too. I sat on the pavement and sobbed. That was the day I learned that you should ALWAYS have a few essentials in your hand luggage.

LAST BUT NOT LEAST

When I write my final, final list I put it on top of the case and tick things off ONLY once they have gone in. It's all too easy to forget those last-minute things that you might still be using right up to the point when you leave – toothbrush, charger, house keys! It's always the things that are really obvious when you are tired or in a rush.

'In particular, always check your passport is up to date. Been there and got that horrific T-shirt.'

Unravel a chain

No matter how carefully I put my necklaces away, I still struggle to avoid those exasperating knots. I swear that sometimes it's a mystery how they get in there, but it goes without saying that the finer the chain, the harder it can be to undo them. Hugely fiddly, requiring patience and dexterity (often in short supply), this is absolutely one of those things that needs to be done slowly and steadily or you'll just end up making it worse.

The best implement to use is ... a pin (or needle). The fine tip is perfect for gently getting into the heart of the knot. Put the chain on a hard surface and wiggle the pin slowly and gently to loosen the knot and then use a second pin (or your fingers) from there. Always undo the clasp before you start.

If the knots are being particularly stubborn you can dab them with a couple of drops of baby oil, olive oil, or some baby powder to help lubricate them. Just make sure you clean the chain thoroughly (but gently) once you're done.

I wear loads of necklaces together at one time, I love them, and the trick to stop them tangling together when you wear them is to put them on one by one and then take them off one by one in the same order.

HOW TO

Build a fire

Whether it's a campfire, a bonfire, a fire pit, a chiminea, or a log burner, knowing how to build and light a fire efficiently and safely is a great life skill to have.

First things first: for all of the above, make sure your wood is dry. If it's damp or wet you'll get a lot of smoke but not much else.

1 Start small. You will need a little dry tinder – that's any combustible material, such as dried grass, leaves, scrunched-up paper, or cardboard.

2 Arrange some kindling (small twigs, dry pine cones) around the tinder. I find the easiest way to build a camp fire from here is to construct a pyramid of small pieces of wood around my tinder, then light the centre and the sides.

3 Once the kindling catches and the fire takes you can start to add bigger logs. The fire needs oxygen to burn so it's important to give it the space it needs to catch.

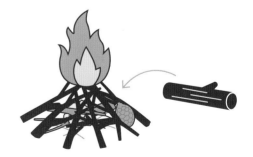

- If you are outdoors, surround your fire with stones or rocks to create a barrier and stop it spreading.

- Never, ever use an accelerant. If you need a bit of help to get it going, you can use cardboard, paper, dry grass, or commercial firelighters, but never pour a flammable liquid onto your fire. It can have fatal consequences.

- Log burners vary, so follow the manufacturer's instructions – and make sure you get your chimney swept regularly! Again, I use the pyramid or tepee formation with my logs. Incidentally, when I got my non-functioning chimney swept (which was fun, like we were in *Oliver Twist*), the breeze that blew down it was so strong that the sweep suggested I get professional insulation OR use a black bin bag full of loosely scrunched-up newspaper and shove it up the chimney to block the draught! The bin bag is still there now! But obviously ONLY do this if your fireplace is ornamental (like ours). It would be really dangerous in a chimney used for a real fire.

- It goes without saying, but keep small children and pets away from any type of fire at all times.

I honed my fire-making technique on I'm A Celebrity. My job in the jungle was to make the rice and build the fire; I didn't want the one job that everybody else wanted, which was to cook. I had zero interest in how to make emu steaks and cook ostrich eggs.

The principles then were exactly as above: collect the kindling; make sure you don't start off with a big chunky piece of wood – lots of people wanted to do that; make sure it's all super dry and that the air can get to it. And that's it. It's very simple to get it started and you can just build up from there. I really enjoyed collecting the kindling in the jungle as there wasn't that much else to do, and to this day I'll be out and about and think, ooh, that would be good for a fire, and that would be good for a fire …

Dry out your phone after dropping it in the loo

I have done this SO many times. In fact, I once managed a double whammy – microphone pack in my right pocket, phone in my left pocket, both down the loo. I didn't know which one to save first! It's all too easy to do.

So if your phone ends up in a toilet bowl, this is what to do:

1   Sounds obvious, but get it out as quickly as you can. The longer it's in there, the more opportunity there is for water to get into all the bits it shouldn't.

2   If your phone is off, don't turn it on. It's very tempting to check to see whether it still works, but this can cause short circuits and mean there's no hope of recovery. Don't do it! If your phone is on, you should turn it off. This is slightly risky in that you will effectively 'wake' the phone in order to power it down, but the alternative is to leave it in sleep mode, in which case any calls or notifications will do the same every time they come through. DON'T plug it in.

3   If it's in a case, take that off and then dry the phone carefully with a soft cloth. Shake it gently to dislodge any water that might be trapped in sockets and ports – the gentle part is key: you don't want to risk any water in there travelling to other parts of the phone.

'This is where "slow and steady wins the race" comes into its own.'

4   Now you need to get any remaining water out of the phone. There's no quick fix (putting it somewhere warm to dry out risks damaging it further). This is where 'slow and steady wins the race' comes into its own.

5   Rice (uncooked!) and lots of it is the best thing to use as it absorbs moisture and will help draw out any drops remaining inside your phone. Fill a large bowl or box and make sure the phone is covered completely. You should leave it for 24 hours minimum – ideally up to 72 hours. This is not easy to do, but be patient – if you get it back in one piece at the end of this it will have been worth it.

Oh yes – and my top tip is never to put your phone in your back pocket when you're going to the loo in the first place!

Recognize the major planets/constellations

I was taught that stars twinkle because they are so far away from the Earth and the atmosphere can disturb their light, and planets shine because they are closer.

But as planets have always been my thing (remember Planets Club? Like I said, I was and still am a total astronomy geek), I suggest the following instead:

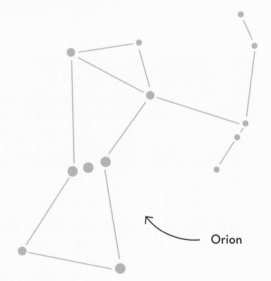

Orion

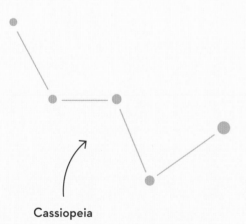

Cassiopeia

1   Start with the moon as your focal point. Ideally, in winter, when it's often easier to see things such as Venus, which is so bright, it's like a torch in the sky.

2   Mars has a pink tinge to it, so that's another easy one to start with. Once you know where to begin it's easier to recognize the planets, which are generally the ones that are too big to be a star.

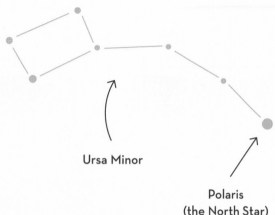

Ursa Minor

Polaris
(the North Star)

Ursa Major,
*aka The Great Bear,
The Plough, or The
Big Dipper*

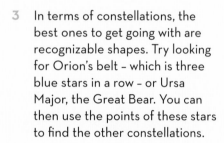

3   In terms of constellations, the best ones to get going with are recognizable shapes. Try looking for Orion's belt – which is three blue stars in a row – or Ursa Major, the Great Bear. You can then use the points of these stars to find the other constellations.

I've found the best way to get the girls interested in the night sky is to share the mythology behind it all. For example, with Cassiopeia, when we look for the distinctive 'W', they love the idea of a queen being so vain for half the year she was made to hang upside down, so we wait to see which way she's hanging. And then if you go to different hemispheres, and you get to see the Southern Cross, it's just wonderful to know that you're looking at light that is thousands of years old. I find it magical. So rather than just saying 'This is the brightest star in the sky', find Ursa Major and Minor and explain that the big bear is up there protecting the baby bear and they're both under a spell. That's way more fun.

About the author

Musician, presenter, businesswoman, and mother, Myleene Klass is one of the UK's most respected and well-loved personalities.

She encountered music at a young age and quickly became one of the most prolific musical talents in the UK on violin, piano, and harp. Myleene made her West End debut in *Miss Saigon* before she was picked up from thousands of others to become one of the five members of the pop group Hear'Say. After the group disbanded, Myleene decided to go back to her roots and recorded a classical album.

Myleene has presented, and appeared on, many TV shows, including *The Classical Brits*, *Loose Women*, *The One Show* and *I'm a Celebrity... Get Me Out of Here!* She has also hosted popular radio shows on Classic FM and Smooth FM, and recently presented a critically acclaimed documentary on miscarriage for UKTV's W channel.

@myleeneklass
@myleeneklass
@KlassMyleene

Index

Thank you

Mum and Dad. Well done, Cutty Sark! You gave me the tools and showed me how to use them. All of this is because of you.
Danke vielmals.
Mahal kita. x

Jessie and Don. You lived most of these with me! I love you both. x

HarperCollins, for publishing this book. Knowledge is indeed (em)powering.

Kate Fox, for the foresight and determination to get this done, written, and published. Thank you for your guidance and belief in this book.

Rose Sandy, for picking up the reins, but not missing a beat. Thank you for your incredible work ethic and organization. I made my deadlines!

Cari Rosen, it was an honour to work with you. I've loved every minute. Thank you for helping organize my thoughts into some kind of order, for always being ready to spring into action, even in the middle of the night, when we mamas get the real work done, and for teaching me Russian!

Severine Berman, the family I choose and love. Thank you for always cracking on and, ultimately, believing in me. None of this would happen without you.

Simon Jones PR, for twenty years of looking out for me and my tribe. The 'How to put out a Fire' section is for you.

Ava, Hero, and Apollo, my beautiful babies. You are the reason I do what I do. I am so proud to be your mama. Thank you for all that you teach me. I love you. Catch the kisses. Madré xxx

Sim, my person, thank you for everything you do for our children and me – my one-man hype team. We are all so lucky to have you. The 'What to do when lost' is for you. To the Slab. x

Ollie and Lini, thank you for making the Klotsons so awesome! From Big Leenie.

The Muthaship, my management, for your continued, relentless hard work, your belief in me, and utter fearlessness, smashing through the glass ceiling every day. Everyone seems to have 'Yes men', but I have a 'No woman', and it bloody well works! Thank you.

Hanah Ovenstone, most of the things in this book I've done with you holding the tool bag or ladder.

Cuz John Cross and Gareth 'Gaga' Thistleton, the Uncles, for your love, guidance, and being a constant to us.

Bradley and Joe Pickering-Taylor, for dragging us up, and being super handy with building houses, make-up brushes, and glue guns alike.

Carryl Thomas, the one-woman dynamo. Thank you for being a solid, measured, and informed voice in our lives.

Lola Belen, for supporting us, loving us, and correcting my Tagalog.

Miss Dorothy 'Babs' Wright, my piano teacher. I miss you.

Lauren Laverne, Graeme Fisher, Vanesa Guallar, Katie Birtwistle, Pippa Nightingale MBE, Karin Darnell, Lisa Laudat, Kate Halfpenny, Michelle Agboulos, Julie Armstrong, Jarmila Mazana, Natasha Hambi, Nikki Bull, Lee Gray, Faebian Averies, Dolapo Tenenbaum, Nazli Shepperd Alizadeh, Jeremy Fine, and Arianne Merry – thank you for everything.

Finally, to those who've taught me so much along the way: Save the Children; and St John Ambulance, especially Matt Atkinson, for your fact-checking and making sure the Klass girls interlock their fingers correctly!

HQ
An imprint of HarperCollinsPublishers Ltd
1 London Bridge Street
London SE1 9GF

www.harpercollins.co.uk

HarperCollinsPublishers
1st Floor, Watermarque Building
Ringsend Road Dublin 4
Ireland

10 9 8 7 6 5 4 3 2 1

First published in Great Britain by
HQ, an imprint of HarperCollinsPublishers Ltd 2022

ISBN: 978-0-00-846791-3

MIX
Paper from
responsible sources
FSC
www.fsc.org   FSC™ C007454

This book is produced from independently certified FSC™ paper
to ensure responsible forest management.

For more information visit:
www.harpercollins.co.uk/green

Printed and bound in the United Kingdom by Bell & Bain

Photography: Mark Hayman & Myleene Klass
Design and illustrations: Louise Evans
Publishing Director: Rose Sandy
Senior Editor: Nira Begum
Senior Production Controller: Halema Begum